Be Born in Us Today

John Davies was Bishop of Shrewsbury from 1987 to 1994. Previously, he spent many years in rural parish and city university ministry in South Africa, Wales and England. He is a former principal of the College of the Ascension in Birmingham and a Residentiary Canon of St Asaph Cathedral.

The author of numerous books and Bible study guides, he is now retired and lives near Llangollen, North Wales. He is a member of the local council, and with his wife Shirley is an associate of the Iona Community.

He is the author of *Crisis of the Cross*, also published by the Canterbury Press.

Be Born in Us Today

The message
of the
Incarnation for today

John Davies

with paintings by
Gillian Bell-Richards

CANTERBURY
PRESS

Norwich

First published in 1999 by The Canterbury Press
Norwich (a publishing imprint of
Hymns Ancient & Modern Limited,
a registered charity),
St Mary's Works, St Mary's Plain,
Norwich, Norfolk, NR3 3BH

British Library Cataloguing in Publication Data

A catalogue record for this book is available
from the British Library

ISBN 1-85311-320-4

Typeset by Rowland Phototypesetting,
Bury St Edmunds, Suffolk
Printed in Great Britain by
Biddles Ltd, Guildford and King's Lynn

This book is dedicated to
The Alei Gefen Chorus of Tel Aviv, Israel

This Choir derives its origins from the tragic history of Central Europe and the former USSR in this century. Most of its members have come to Israel from Russia in recent years. In the setting of the Israel of today, in the homeland of Jesus, it stands for the power of choral music to bring together Jew and Arab, Jew and Christian, in a sharing of pain and hope. It embodies a hope for peace and justice – for shalom – in the tradition of the Ten Commandments given through Moses. In this way, it lives by a spirit similar to that which inspired the struggle against apartheid in South Africa, an experience which at many points informs my account of the Scriptures in this book.

The Choir works to international professional standards, but is committed to maintaining an amateur status. Among its many ventures, it has been a distinguished participant in the Llangollen International Musical Eisteddfod in North Wales, which is one of the most effective instruments of peace-making and reconcilliation created in Britain since 1945.

By this dedication, I am not trying to suggest that members of the Choir would agree with every sentence in this book. But I feel that the Choir does represent two basic convictions which Christianity inherits from Judaism: first, that theology, to be true to its nature, requires not only to be discussed but to be acted out in the struggle for justice and peace; and, secondly, as the opening chapters of Luke's Gospel make clear, a true theology requires not only to be studied but to be sung.

I am very grateful to Christine Smith, Publisher of the Canterbury Press, for introducing me to Gillian Bell-Richards of Hereford, who has provided the pictures for this book.

These pictures are not mere 'illustrations' of my written text. For one thing, they were painted before my text was written and we had never heard of each other until after the completion of the text. But also – and this is more important – they are statements in their own right, communicating truth far more directly and sharply than I can express with words. I feel that my text is greatly privileged to be in partnership with these pictures. The pictures, in their medium, and the written words, in their medium, converge in the common purpose of seeking to recognize what we are asking for when we pray, 'Be Born in us Today'.

I am also grateful to the members of various groups, especially in the Llangollen area, who have patiently and creatively worked on several of these studies with me.

JOHN DAVIES
Epiphany 1999
Froncysyllte

Contents

List of illustrations:

Foreword

These meditations on the Christmas stories will come as a refreshing surprise to all who think there isn't much new to say on the subject. But their freshness comes from the clarity and vividness with which John Davies makes the connection with the here and now of exclusion, debt, the paralysis of traditional clerical religion and so on. These are wonderfully *persuasive* reflections, gently and firmly leading us to clear recognition: Jesus was not born into a different world from our own. And the transformations set out in the Christmas stories are the transformations required from us and offered to us.

† Rowan Williams
Monmouth

Introduction

Making Christmas Connections

My first Christmas as a parish priest was in 1957, in a parish measuring sixty miles by ninety, consisting of about sixteen congregations, in South Africa's rural Eastern Transvaal. At the centre of the parish there was a new gold mine. At this mine, there was a compound or barracks, accommodating several thousand African men. These were mostly migrant workers on nine-month contracts, drawn from countries and tribes all over Southern and Central Africa. A faithful Anglican congregation had formed, mainly by the efforts of some mineworkers who were voluntary catechists. Normally, we met in a schoolroom of the mine's training department. But this section was all locked up over Christmas. So, for our midnight Eucharist, we met in a room which was used by the men themselves as a general domestic room. It had no electricity; by night it was home to a few dozen fowls belonging to the men. My most abiding memory of that Christmas is of a candle-lit congregation singing the praises of the coming of Christ in half-a-dozen different languages, accompanied by the intermittent complaints of poultry whose sleep-pattern had been so strangely disturbed.

My understanding of the meaning of Christmas now owes a great deal to that occasion. Let me mention some of the connections, as I see them, with the stories in the Gospels.

1. It happened in a borrowed room, an annexe to a public meeting-place.

2. It was a hidden event, not publicized much in advance.

3. It happened in the dark. Few people saw or understood what was happening; most were asleep. (Martin Luther King used to tell of Rip Van Winkle, who went to sleep when George III's flag flew over North America, and woke up after George Washington had become President; he had been 'sleeping through a revolution'; this phrase has become, for me, one of the most profound descriptions of what was happening, over many apparently fruitless years, in South Africa.)

4. It happened in the company of farmyard creatures, humanity's close companions. These live birds were, in their own way, part of the offertory and the song of creation.

5. What actually happened – the sharing of bread and wine – was like the birth at Bethlehem; it was inconspicuous, unspectacular. Either this has something to do with God, or it has no particular significance at all.

6. It happened among people who were poor and vote-less non-citizens. They were not 'simple' or 'ordinary' people; most of them were people of valuable skill and courage in the dangers of the gold-mining industry; but they were people of no status within the systems controlled by the political and economic dominances of the day.

7. It was an occasion which affirmed the eternal value of people who otherwise were counted as having little value; each communicant was receiving, individually and personally, the body and blood of Christ – Son of God and Son of Mary – 'given for YOU'.

8. It was an occasion which affirmed the value of material things; bread and alcoholic drink could both be sources of argument and fighting and killing; but here they were being claimed as ways for God to be present among people.

9. It was an occasion which brought people together from many different backgrounds, from an immense area of the world. It overcame their separateness but honoured their distinctiveness. White people on the mine used to think that the 'language problem' could be solved by using the common language of the mines, Fanagalo. But Fanagalo was an artificial language forced on the people by the employers; it did not speak to the hearts of anyone, and was useless as a language of devotion and prayer. So we sang in five or six languages at the same time, using the same melodies. I led the

service in Zulu; I preached in English; this was translated by Mr Ernest Zibi, sentence by sentence, into Xhosa, and by Mr Desmond Qobela Joel into seSotho, and by Mr Azariah Zandamela into Shangaan. So we communicated to all in their own languages. Language was a problem only if we saw it as a problem.

10. So there were words; there was speech. But the event did not depend on words. The words of the liturgy were formal and not very personal; the words of the preacher were fumbling and incompetent. The real heart of the occasion was the celebration of the word made flesh, Christ being present in the material things of food and drink, of a shared feast and of us being a group of people together.

11. The congregation was an international fellowship of poor workers. By the law of the land and by the assumptions of the employers, they should have been kept apart, in ethnic or tribal groups. The Church provided the occasion for them to be together in a situation where such bodies as trade unions were not permitted. This was a defiance of the official systems, not by violence but by recognizing a truth which the official systems refused to acknowledge.

12. As a church, we knew that we were part of a community of defiance. We heard very carefully what our bishops and other leaders were saying, in confronting the system of apartheid with the values of the gospel. But we were not trying to make out that everything was

the fault of other people. We were part of a movement of repentance; our confession of sin was an essential part of our approach to the God who was coming among us.

13. In the midst of the darkness, the defiance, the protest, the poverty, the injustice, this was a celebration; it was about joy, pleasure, dignity, glory.

14. All of us were people far from home. Members of the congregation were victims of political and economic systems in which they had no power or voice; they were exiles, or migrant workers. In the law of the land, they had practically no rights. Some were from other areas of South Africa; but they were exiles in their own land.

15. 'Herod' and 'Caesar' were part of our landscape. The whole land was under an alien colonial authority. The ultimate political authority was far away, in London. The actual effective government of the country was in a very uneasy relationship with the ultimate authority, and was much more cruel than the ultimate authority would have wished. In the bargaining and jostling for power between the two authorities, people like our mine-workers got the rawest of raw deals.

16. The mine-workers were enrolled and enumerated, for statistical and taxation purposes. They each carried their number on an indestructible wrist-band. They were like human beef. They had no bargaining power; their working conditions of health and safety were secured

by the interests of the employers. But their actual labour was entirely for the wealth of the mine-owners, and they had no more actual say concerning pay and conditions than if they had been slaves.

17. As in the days of Jesus, we were surrounded by a hubbub of political argument. There were many different voices, many different remedies being offered, many different ways of allocating blame for all that was wrong. But this event, inconspicuous and politically insignificant though it was, took place because oppressed and voiceless people took an initiative themselves and did their own organizing.

18. In the neighbouring countryside, 'innocents' were being massacred. There was terrible infant mortality, caused directly by political decisions concerning housing and water-supply for local African communities. As a parish priest, I had responsibility for funerals; I had to deal with families where babies were dying because of institutionalized cruelty. The worst time of the year was from Christmas to February.

19. One of our most committed members was a carpenter, a local builder. He was Mr Wynand Lee. He and his family were what the South African system called 'coloured' people. His wife, Mrs Lee, was midwife for virtually all the African babies of the area. Mr Lee had a heart of gold. He worked on the mine and gave much voluntary service among the African communities around. They were a wonderful couple, friends to us all.

20. Like the Gospel-writers, we treated people's ancestral names, or surnames, with respect. I have mentioned the names of a few of the black people who were involved with our congregation. As far as most of the whites, and the employers, were concerned, these people would be known merely as 'Ernest' or 'Desmond' or 'Maria'; they were mere 'natives', referred to as 'boy' or 'girl', as individual workers or servants with no family or background. In the Church, they were recognized as people who each had a community identity, a tradition, an inheritance in an ancestry. By modern Western standards, we were very formal. Even when we knew each other well, we were 'Mrs Lee', 'Mr Zibi', 'Mr Zandamela'. A person's surname is part of their dignity, part of an identity which powerful and secure authorities should not treat lightly. In Zulu, when we greet each other, we are greeting each other's ancestors, the communities of the living and the dead whom we represent. The Gospel stories treat such names with care.

21. As in the Gospels, the role and contribution of women were vital. The great majority of our congregation on the mine were men, because of the contract labour system. But there were a few women, whose contribution was far more significant than their numbers would have suggested. Most were fairly old, but one or two were younger. They supported each other across the generations, in a heavily male-dominated situation. Legally, they were probably the most insecure group of all; but all the rest depended on them.

22. In the Gospels, some of the most interesting things occur to old people who just happen to be hanging around. When our congregation on the mine started to meet, it was joined by a few old African people from farms nearby; officially, they were not supposed to be allowed into the compound. But nobody seemed to notice a couple of old people hovering around. They had simply been waiting, waiting for years for the Church to notice that they existed.

23. When we met for the Christmas Eucharist that midnight, it was a new thing. Nothing like it had ever happened before in that place.

24. Gold had its curious place in our story. This event happened on a gold mine. Gold was the environment. The human and environmental and economic cost of this mineral extraction was obvious all around. Gold was the one reason for all of us being there. The place was organized by the will of the super-rich, with their complex and obscure sciences of geology and economics. Somehow, this exploitative and arcane enterprise was, through its poorest agents, meeting its Lord.

25. At our Eucharist, we were not far off from using a manger. We used an ordinary table, which had been sat on by the hens, for the eucharistic altar. We used the things provided by the world around. We used mealie-cobs in place of charcoal for incense.

26. The first two chapters of Luke's Gospel are just one

song after another. So with us. To sing the praises of the Son of God, we used the one instrument given to all of us, the human voice; no other instrument. I consulted Mr Lee on the question of whether we should sing the liturgy or say it. I remember very clearly his wise answer. 'If you sing the service, you exclude those who can't sing: if you say the service, you exclude those who can't read. If you sing the service, those who can't read may perhaps only be able to sing la la la; but that will be their worship and God will understand it.' So we sang the service, and the less educated members were not disabled by the literate ones.

27. Those who cannot read have long memories, not just of their own experience but of the experience of those who have gone before. These people remembered and treasured the stories of the old heroes of their communities, stories hidden from the literate academic historians. It must have been because of what the Gospel-writers heard from people of this kind, people with this kind of memory and this kind of interest in story-telling, that we now have the written narrative in our hands.

28. 'Jesus' was the name which we could all recognize, which drew us together. There were many languages, and therefore many different words for 'God'. But God is recognizable among human beings in the human name 'Jesus'. 'Jesus' is recognizable across the different languages. If you can recognize the two sounds 'Jesus' and 'Amen', you can find your way and participate in

Christian worship. So we decided to name our polyglot congregation 'The Church of the Holy Name of Jesus'.

29. Although we were at the other end of Africa, we were in the same continent which gave hospitality to Jesus and his parents when they were escaping from terror at home; we were a small part of Africa's continuing privilege of providing a place for the Son of God to reside.

30. Towards the end of our midnight celebration, a light shower of rain started to fall. The sound of rain on a tin roof always adds something to worship, either to give it a bit of a lift, or to drown it completely. This rain on our roof was not exactly an echo of the voices of angels, but it did sound remarkably like distant bells. And in that part of the world, rain is a blessing and an occasion of joy – a wonderful thing to happen at a wedding! Clouds, as well as stars, can have their place in the celebration of God's arrival in our world.

For me, these are all connections between the Gospel nativity stories and my own experience. This book is an invitation to readers and study-groups to make similar connections for themselves. My experience happens to have been in a particular situation in South Africa. But all the ingredients are to be found in other places. They are certainly to be found in Britain; but they may be found in unexpected places, places far from the centres of power and privilege, places with few obvious signs of either peace or glory.

The nativity stories are about God coming into our world and claiming it as his own. They are written, for the original readers and for us, to enable us to make these connections for ourselves. This is not just a literary exercise. The whole purpose is to help us to recognize God's manner of being in his world, and to help us to discover God's presence in our world, so that we can be more effective and obedient disciples in our own place and our own day. I have found these stories to be fruitful for this purpose, as you will perhaps realize from the thirty examples which I have given; all of them derive directly from various elements in the Gospel narratives. I hope that this may suggest the purpose of this study, rather better than a theoretical exposition. I have no doubt that I could find other connections, if my memory were better. These have stuck in my mind, not just as sentimental recollections, but because these aspects of our Lord's nativity have turned out to be valuable and fruitful for me, in trying to respond to God's calling within a particular set of circumstances.

The experience of South Africa, and especially of that mine-congregation, changed Christmas for me, from a childhood memory and a liturgical duty, into a celebration of God's defiance of the power-systems of the world and a greeting of God's claim upon us as disciples and worshippers.

This recollection of mine may open a window on the process of writing the nativity stories of the Gospels. All the thirty little details that I have given are, in some way, history. But they are very slanted history. They are very selective. They are written down over forty years after the event. They are not recorded anywhere else. There will be no reference to that Christmas gathering in the archives of the mine administration, or in those of the Magisterial District of Bethal in the Transvaal. There are all sorts of assumptions in what I have written. If that gathering is remembered at all by anyone else, it will be remembered in one way by Mr Zandamela, and in a quite different way by the Manager of the Compound, Mr Prinsloo. I have recorded the event because of its meaning for me. I cannot be sure that my understanding of the regulations concerning the use of mine property is correct, or that I have remembered accurately the conditions on which non-mine-employees were allowed on to the site. I cannot even be sure what sorts of bread and wine were used, or what the sermon was about. But my purpose is not to give a specimen of the social history of the mine, but to give an account of what I believe to have been an example of God's presence in the world. On that basis, and only on that basis, judge my story. Similarly, we do not go to Luke to get details of the Roman taxation system, or to Matthew to get astronomical information. We go to find something concerning the meaning and manner of God's presence in the world.

I hope that this little book may help readers and study-groups to make similar kinds of connections between the Bible and the world in which they find themselves today.

We shall be concerned with the stories in the Gospels according to Matthew and Luke which centre on the birth of Christ. Immediately, we face an interesting and curious fact. Although Christmas has become the most popular festival in the Christian calendar, and the Millennium celebrates the 2000th anniversary of Jesus' birth, many of the first Christian communities were apparently not interested in these events at all. For the authors Paul and Mark and John, Jesus started to be of interest only when he was an adult. Only in Matthew and Luke is there any direct reference to our Lord's infancy; and their stories do not easily fit together. There must have come a time when Christians started to say 'We are grateful for all that we have been told about the adult ministry of Jesus. But how did it all begin? What went on behind the scenes in the formation of this person whom we acknowledge as Saviour?' And so our nativity stories came to be written. But the reason was not a sentimental interest in babyhood, nor did it arise out of a desire to spin fairy-tale yarns. That sort of thing came later, when writers started telling fantastic tales of Jesus as a child miracle-worker who was quite unrecognizable as a human being, as one of us. But the reason for these nativity stories in the Gospels was to help Christians to answer the question, 'How does God act and show his presence in the world? What do we look for? How are we to recognize God, so that we can share in his activity and respond to his calling? What would be the signs that God is doing something new, in our day and in our place?' These are questions which Christian disciples need to ask in every age and in every place. We shall find that Matthew and Luke were quite right to feel that the Gospel would be incomplete if there was no account of the beginnings of the presence of the Son of God in the world. And that means that we are right to celebrate Christmas.

One reason for the popularity of Christmas is that it connects with our own experience of family, childhood and domestic anxieties. We identify with the Christmas stories more easily than with some of the other stories in the Gospels. And that is another reason for us to value what Matthew and Luke have given us. For instance, I recall being told that I was named after John the Baptist. I was the only child of my mother, who was 39 years old when I was born; my father, a quiet conservative Anglican priest, was nearly 50. Widows were important in my childhood; I knew both my grandmothers, but my grandfathers had both died thirty years before I was born. Many readers will find personal connections of this sort. Do not ignore them. Details of this kind represent the reality of God's presence in the world in the person of Jesus. We say that God was in Christ. This is theologically known as the doctrine of the incarnation, and is right at the heart of the Christian message. The doctrine would be true even if we did not have the nativity stories; but these stories make the doctrine real for us. In St John's phrase, the Word became flesh; these stories give flesh to the doctrine. And for this purpose it is the human points of contact that matter, rather than the more supernatural and mysterious elements. For most of us, this is what Christmas is mainly about.

But Christmas is not the beginning of the story. Most biographies start by telling us something about the background of the subject's parents, and probably of the grandparents as well. It is difficult for a biographer to

make a good start if the subject was born of uninteresting parents and in a dull period of history. The parents of
Jesus were certainly not uninteresting, and the historical
situation was anything but dull. But Luke has little to
tell us about Jesus' father, and zero about Jesus' grandparents. On the other hand, he has a great deal to tell
us about the parents and background of a fairly distant
cousin. Luke's starting-point is with Zechariah and
Elizabeth; and we are told more about these two than
about any other married couple in the Bible. Of all the
Gospel-writers, Luke is the one who comes closest to
giving us a 'Life of Jesus'. But he is not an ordinary
biographer. His purpose is not just to supply interesting
information but to equip disciples for their task. That
is why he starts where he does. That is the purpose
which causes him to choose what to tell; that also is the
purpose which will enable us to claim and use the stories
which he and Matthew have given to us.

If this is the kind of purpose that we bring to these
stories, it will be on these lines that we shall value them.
I do not propose to take much time on problems of
historical accuracy.[1] We are dealing with stories concerning the origins of the Christian faith; and origins
are usually hidden, fragile, easily obscured. The first
living creatures left few fossils. These stories of Matthew
and Luke are, for the most part, supported by no other
evidence. The two evangelists show no sign of knowing
each other's texts, and the two texts do not fit together
very neatly. But they are both concerned about a fundamental set of issues. They are both, in different ways,
concerned to show how in Christ there is a divine

identity and a human identity. They both work with the question of how Jesus was born in Bethlehem but actually came from Nazareth. They both find ways of stressing how Jesus as Son of God was recognized by unexpected people and ignored by the respectable. So there are deep areas of fundamental agreement between the two writers, and these are more significant than the differences between them. So, in this study-programme, we shall try to concentrate on the issues which seem to have been of most interest to the Gospel-writers. We shall pursue such questions as:

- What did the text mean to the writer?

- In what way did the writer think that the story was going to be of interest and value to the church for which he was writing?

- In what ways does the story help us in our own attempts to discover God with us in our world?

- How does the story encourage us or warn us, as we try to be a community of disciples in our own time and place?

- How fruitful and helpful is this story as an indication of the manner of God's presence in the world, so that the disciple-community can recognize God's presence and work with it?

- If this is how God was then, how is God now?

These are the purposes for which the Gospel is written; if we are praying that Christ will be born in us today, then let us be alert for the implications of him being thus born in us. Let us watch for the signs of his coming and the marks of his presence.

How to Use this Book

This book is intended to help Christians to use the nativity stories in the Gospels as a way of renewing their faith and discipleship. In this sense, it is intended to serve the same purpose for which the stories were originally written. The important thing for readers, whether they are on their own or with a group, is to let the story make connections with their own experience and their own situation. No one else can do this for you. You are the expert on your own experience. All that a book like this can do is to offer a few hints. I will be suggesting some questions, but the most valuable questions will be those which come out of your own situation.

Group work

A group which intends to work with this book might well spread its meetings out across several months. In the Church's calendar, the stories covered in this book start at the end of March, with the festival of the Annunciation, and finish at the beginning of February, with Candlemas. There is, of course, no need to be tied to those dates; but there is a whole series of festivals and commemorations which recall events in these stories, and one of the effects of a work-group in a parish might be that new life could be breathed into the liturgy and the symbolism of these festivals. In the suggestions for group-work, there are several references to this sort of possibility.

In preparation for a meeting, members could be asked to read the relevant chapter of this book in advance. At the meeting itself, the text of the story may be read aloud, with different readers taking the different parts of the story-telling and dialogue. *The Dramatised Bible* text is supplied for this purpose in this book; it is a most valuable resource, and can really help to let the narrative come alive. It is mainly based on the *Good News Bible*; that is only one of several accessible versions which are available; members of a study-group would be well-advised to bring other versions with them to the meeting for comparison, such as the *New Revised Standard Version*.

Before going into the specific questions printed, it would be useful if members could be given time to tell the group what particular point of interest strikes them, what connections they see between the story in the Gospel and their own experience.

The fundamental question, throughout, should be this:

If this is what happened when God was taking flesh in the coming of Jesus Christ, how is God taking flesh in our world and in our flesh now? What is the meaning of this story for our obedience as followers of Jesus now? In what ways does this story alert us to recognize the presence of God in his world now?

There are three or four questions supplied for most of the following chapters. It is probably best not to try to tackle all of them with the whole group. If your group is of six or more people, break up into three or four teams, one question to each team. After about fifteen minutes, let each team send one or two representatives to another team and offer their ideas and conclusions to the other team, returning to their original team after another ten minutes or so. In this way, each person should get a thorough discussion on one question and some idea of at least two others. And everyone will get an opportunity to put their ideas into words.

This book is in ten chapters. But the use of it in groups need not be limited to ten meetings. Some chapters have more suggestions for group-work than others; you may well feel that you should take more than one meeting for some of these chapters. This part of the New Testament can be very fruitful for our understanding of our calling as disciples in our own day, and we should not tie ourselves down too tightly to a programme.

I hope, also, that readers who do not belong to study-groups will nevertheless look at the questions, and see whether the questions can lead them on in their discipleship.

Perhaps your group could appoint someone to act as a note-taker – not to record everything that everyone says, but to note specific matters which could be put together at the end of the series of meetings, as recommendations, ideas, matters for further consideration, requests to other groups, etc. (See paragraph 2 of the group work suggestions after Chapter 10.)

One last point about group work with this book: there is both a blessing and a problem in the fact that the central stories are very well known indeed. In any representative Christian group, there will be some people who passionately love these stories and all the symbols and customs which are familiar at Christmas, and who may be upset at the thought of anything that seems new or disturbing. And there will probably be others who are weary of what seems to them to be sentimentality or unreality or commercialism, and who like to have an opportunity to debunk the whole thing. The book will, I hope, give plenty of opportunity to those who want to think the stories through, in a critical way. But it is no accident that these stories have so firmly grasped human hearts and imaginations. Let both types of people really listen to each other, and stay with each other, as they work with these stories. And let those who greatly value the tradition realize the force of the words which are both the title of the book and its purpose and its prayer, 'Be born in us *today*'. Today is not yesterday; and it is not 2000 years ago, either.

For prayer and reflection

I have supplied suggestions for prayer after each chapter. These are prayers and reflections which I happen to have found helpful. There is, of course, an immense supply of prayers, poems, songs and carols, which have been inspired by the stories concerning Christ's nativity. If you find the prayers in this book useful, fine. If not, do not be bound by them. If you do use them, please do not simply make them a quick glance to God at the end of a meeting before saying goodbye. Take time for any praying of this kind. Use words in prayer only if you have to. The incarnation of the Son of God took place in darkness and silence – 'All things were lying in peace and silence, and night in her swift course was half spent, when your all-powerful word leapt from your royal throne in heaven . . .' (Wisdom 18:14). Your silence together may be a much truer way than any words into closeness with the God who comes to us in Jesus.

1

The Annunciation to Zechariah
Luke 1:5–25

Narrator 1 During the time when Herod was king of Judaea, there was a priest named Zechariah, who belonged to the priestly order of Abijah. His wife's name was Elizabeth; she also belonged to a priestly family.

Narrator 2 They both lived good lives in God's sight and obeyed fully all the Lord's laws and commands. They had no children because Elizabeth could not have any, and she and Zechariah were both very old.

Narrator 1 One day Zechariah was doing his work as a priest in the Temple, taking his turn in the daily service.

Narrator 2 According to the custom followed by the priests, he was chosen by lot to burn incense on the altar.

Narrator 1 So he went into the Temple of the Lord, while the crowd of people outside prayed during the hour when the incense was burnt. An angel of the Lord appeared to him, standing on the right of the altar where the incense was burnt. When Zechariah saw him, he was alarmed and felt afraid. But the angel said to him:

Angel	Don't be afraid, Zechariah! God has heard your prayer, and your wife Elizabeth will bear you a son. You are to name him John. How glad and happy you will be, and how happy many others will be when he is born! He will be a great man in the Lord's sight. He must not drink any wine or strong drink. From his very birth he will be filled with the Holy Spirit, and he will bring back many of the people of Israel to the Lord their God. He will go ahead of the Lord, strong and mighty like the prophet Elijah. He will bring fathers and children together again; he will turn disobedient people back to the way of thinking of the righteous; he will get the Lord's people ready for him.
Narrator 1	Zechariah said to the angel:
Zechariah	How shall I know if this is so? I am an old man, and my wife is old also.
Angel	I am Gabriel. I stand in the presence of God, who sent me to speak to you and tell you this good news. But you have not believed my message, which will come true at the right time. Because you have not believed, you will be unable to speak; you will remain silent until the day my promise to you comes true.
Narrator 2	In the meantime the people were waiting for Zechariah and wondering why he was spending such a long time in the Temple.
Narrator 1	When he came out, he could not speak to them, and so they knew that he had seen a vision in the Temple. Unable to say a word, he made signs to them with his hands.
Narrator 2	When his period of service in the Temple was over, Zechariah went back home. Some time later his wife Elizabeth became pregnant and

did not leave the house for nine months. She
said:

Elizabeth   Now at last the Lord has helped me. He has
taken away my public disgrace!

This is where it all begins, in Luke's account of the
gospel. It starts with one elderly couple.

But first we need to notice how Luke pins the story
down at a particular point of history. A lot of the story is
of a kind which cannot be checked against documentary
history, as defined by those who have the power to write
official chronicles. The persons of this drama are all
people who would be counted insignificant by contemporary secular historians. The events may have caught
the attention of a few rural characters, honest enough
individuals, no doubt, but non-voters, people with no
access to the microphones and media-offices of the day.
But the mind of the Christian movement is not necessarily steered by the priorities of secular historians. One
of the most celebrated of recent British historians refused
to recognize the significance of the German resistance
movement against Nazism, on the grounds that it was
'politically impotent'.[1] Yet the witness of this movement
is surely one of the most valuable stories of the human
spirit in this century. By the same argument, the movements of South African students against apartheid thirty
years ago could be described as politically impotent. But
it is from this generation that the present South Africa
is drawing its leaders and ambassadors.

Luke is writing about people who had no political
leverage. But he locates his story at a specific point in

Jewish history. He expects us to take his story seriously, as a series of events which have a genuine basis in history, and he will go on doing this later in his writing. He pins his story down with a political marker – 'in the days of Herod the King' – just as we might say 'when Jack Straw was Home Secretary'.

But, fortunately, our Home Secretary is not simply a modern counterpart of King Herod. Herod did indeed have responsibility for the internal organization of the State of the Jewish people, as an element within a wider administration. But by his reference to Herod, Luke is setting his story in the frame of an ugly and stressful time for the Jewish people. Herod was a clever and vicious local politician, promoted from out of the national community by the colonial power of Rome. Such a figure would incur all the resentment of other members of the subject race; and he would be held in contempt by the foreign power who controlled the natives with an appearance of effortless superiority.

This is the background for our story. There were many groups of people offering different solutions for the nation's problems. There were those who advocated violence and guerilla warfare; there were others who called on people to join them in withdrawing to the desert to wait for the final death of the nation; there were some who urged co-operation with the secular establishment, and others who put their effort into being a kind of moral minority of people who could cure the disorder by superior purity. We can recognize all these types of response in today's world. In the midst of all this discord and blame-throwing there were quiet people who got on with the job of living as best they could, according to the limited opportunities that the situation could give them.

It is from this last group of people that Luke's first real characters are drawn. From the point of view of the Roman administration, Elizabeth and Zechariah would have been just a couple of old fogeys from the native population, who made a particular hobby out of the native religion. For Luke, and for Luke's readers, Elizabeth and Zechariah were both members of priestly families, people who centred their identity and their loyalty on the old values and the established traditions of the nation. Luke stresses that both Elizabeth and Zechariah were people committed to the justice of God's law, and that they did not deviate from God's commandments. As faithful members of the priestly community, they treasured the laws and ordinances which most distinguished Judaism from its pagan environment. These laws were designed to prevent poverty, enslavement and exploitation; they provided for equitable sharing of land and wealth, for equality before the law, and for the systematic sharing of knowledge through education. This structure of God's revealed will was being notoriously overruled by the unbelieving colonial powers which had taken control of the nation. Despite all the turmoil and political upheavals, despite the wounded hopes and deep disappointments of recent years, people like Elizabeth and Zechariah had helped the Jewish nation to remember God's purpose and character. The ritual of the Temple, the initiation of the young, the telling of the old stories, and the reminder of the moral law of God, had all been maintained. Probably, the enthusiasts for one solution or another were impatient with this traditionalism and dismissed it as irrelevant. Luke will have plenty to say later about the fundamental disturbance generated by the child of Elizabeth and Zechariah, and about the deeper disturbance generated by that child's cousin, the son of Mary. But first, Luke shows us that the new movement of the gospel starts within the faithful fulfilment of the requirements of the traditional conventions.

This continues to be the way that Christian obedience happens. The lay Christians, and bishops and priests, who have struggled most courageously for truth and justice in our day, and who have sacrificially stood alongside the poor and oppressed, have often been people of a quite conventional and conservative spirituality. They have stood for traditional values, in opposition to modern novelties like legalized racial discrimination or ethnic cleansing; in their pain and loneliness, they have been sustained by traditional symbolisms, which some Christians in less stressed situations have been eager to discard.

This provides an answer to the question of why Luke starts his story of Christ, not by describing the grandparents of Jesus, or his school-friends, or his domestic life, but by this detailed account of two old people who were only distant relatives, not even sharing the same ancestry as Jesus.

Luke was writing mainly for a Gentile reader and a Gentile Church. By the time that he wrote, the Christian movement had spread quite widely over the Gentile

world. By starting his story with the figures of Herod
and Elizabeth and Zechariah, Luke was stressing to his
Gentile readers that they owed the origins of their faith
to its roots in Judaism. His story has started with Judaism at its best and at its worst. The Christian movement
starts by taking very seriously the culture within which
it is sown. And the dangers to the Christian movement
will come from the elements within that culture, such
as Herod, who themselves are betraying the best of that
culture. Luke will have more to say about the viciousness
of Herod's family as the story develops.

Zechariah, as Luke describes him, is simply a good
priest. He is not a prophet. Prophecy has died, many
generations ago. There is no direct communication from
God, no new word, no fresh inspiration. Decisions have
to be made by means of a lottery. This is all part of the
sadness of the day, the sense that the good times are
long past. And it would seem likely that even the priesthood may die out if other priests are as childless as
Zechariah and Elizabeth.

Zechariah is not a man of great courage or vision.
Privately, he grieves for his failure to become a father.
But one day he has the rare good fortune to be chosen
by the lottery to carry out the supreme function of the
priesthood, to represent the whole nation in the prayer
in the sanctuary. This is the high point of his professional competence. It is a once-in-a-lifetime privilege.
There are 18,000 priests, and the opportunity will not
come his way again. He offers the community's prayers
for national deliverance and for the coming of God's
kingdom. For a few blessed moments he can forget his

private sadness and concentrate on his professional religious role. So he is taken completely off guard when an archangel drops in, confusing all the issues; Gabriel announces that Zechariah's prayers, as the nation's priest, have been heard, and at the same time his domestic sadness is being removed and he is going to be a father.

In these nativity stories, in both Luke and Matthew, there is a lot about communication. God has ways of getting through to people. In some cases, these people may be old and respectable, not the kind of people who easily get carried away by novelties. In other cases, they may be young and immature, the sort of people whom the older would call irresponsible. To both, God can communicate. An 'angel' is a messenger, an agent through whom communication comes.

Zechariah is a responsible, competent priest. But Gabriel is telling him that he is to be father of a prophet; and that is a horse of a very different colour. Zechariah's son, John, is going to pick up the threads from the last of the Hebrew prophets, Malachi. From the very last verse of Malachi's prophecy, Gabriel notes that John's task will be to 'turn the hearts of the fathers to the children' (omitting Malachi's other concern, of turning the hearts of children to their fathers). In other words, God's servant is to enable the older generation to relate to and to identify with the vision and the impatience of the young.

All this is too much for Zechariah, that faithful and conventional old priest. In his confusion, he takes it upon himself to argue with an archangel. 'I'm too old for that sort of thing, and my wife is already coming up to the menopause.' Zechariah is the best that the priesthood can offer. He preserves and cherishes the tradition. But God is not in the business of preservation; God is offering transformation. Zechariah's religion is precious and noble. It values the old, but cannot create the new. Zechariah does not understand the new, and he is unwilling to co-operate with it.

Gabriel has no patience with this. At the risk of seeming peevish, he takes the line that, if the guardian of the old cannot accept the new which is coming, he has to be silenced, at least until the new has arrived. Zechariah is not deprived of his human ability to father a child; but he is deprived of his religious power to bless the people. So, when he eventually comes out of the Temple, he is unable to complete his service. He quickly has to learn to communicate in sign-language. And he goes home. For the nine-month period of her unexpected pregnancy, he will be unable to talk to his wife.

Zechariah has experienced something like what we would nowadays call a stroke. But his enforced silence is part of God's providence. If he cannot willingly accept what God is offering, then he needs to be silent about it. As a priest, especially, he is in a position to communicate and spread misunderstanding. On the far side of the future event, he will be able to speak, to bless, and to praise. But, for now, he is speechless. He has to wait. He has to share in the discipline of waiting, the essential skill in pregnancy. As a priest, as a servant of the liturgy, waiting for God's self-disclosure is supposed to be one of his most professional skills. Although they will not be able to talk together, he and Elizabeth will wait together.

Elizabeth herself goes into seclusion. She keeps her pregnancy a secret, until the evidence for it is impossible to conceal, and the most dangerous time for miscarriage has passed.

Questions for Groups

1. What connections, however apparently unimportant, do you find, between this story and your own experience?

2. Look back on the changes and developments that have taken place in the life of your church or community. How have they come about? What hidden things were going on which later made these developments possible?

3. What kind of people are needed by God to enable change and growth? What kind of acceptance or resistance happens?

4. Is your church primarily in the business of preservation or of transformation? What priorities are suggested by your church's budgeting? Are there times when the priesthood might need to be silenced?

For Prayer and Reflection

I knew Canon T. R. Milford when he was Chancellor
of Lincoln Cathedral. He was a priest of great wisdom, who had spent many years in India. In his
retirement, when he was well over 70 years old, he
started to write poetry. A collection of his poems was
privately published, called *Belated Harvest*. This is
from that collection. It may not be great verse, but
I do not know anything else which expresses this
particular idea. It flows naturally on from the figure
of Zechariah, who at the end of his life had one phase
of universal significance, and then is heard of no
more.

Lines Found on a Workshop Floor

We are the paint that was left on the palette,
  After the painter had found the true shade;
We are the pieces knocked off by the mallet,
  Till the form hid in the stone was displayed.

We are the words that the poet discarded,
  Seeking the one word to finish his line;
We are the people that no one regarded,
  We stayed in shadow that others might shine.

Count us not wasted who thus were expended!
　We pay the cost of creation's employ;
We, in God's purpose no less comprehended,
　Dying in him have our share of his joy.

And pray for us old people, that we may be available
to God for any new things which he wants us to be
involved in.

2

The Annunciation to Mary
Luke 1:26–38

Narrator	In the sixth month, God sent the Angel Gabriel to Nazareth, a town in Galilee, to a virgin pledged to be married to a man named Joseph, a descendant of David. The virgin's name was Mary. The angel went to her and said:
Angel	Greetings, you who are highly favoured! The Lord is with you.
Narrator	Mary was greatly troubled at his words and wondered what kind of greeting this might be. But the angel said to her:
Angel	Do not be afraid, Mary, you have found favour with God. You will be with child and give birth to a son, and you are to give him the name Jesus. He will be great and will be called the Son of the Most High. The Lord God will give him the throne of his father David, and he will reign over the house of Jacob for ever; his kingdom will never end.
Narrator	Mary asked the angel:
Mary	How will this be, since I am a virgin?
Angel	The Holy Spirit will come upon you, and the power of the Most High will overshadow you. So the Holy One to be born will be called the

	Son of God. Even Elizabeth your relative is going to have a child in her old age, and she who was said to be barren is in her sixth month. For nothing is impossible with God.
Narrator	Mary answered:
Mary	I am the Lord's servant. May it be to me as you have said.
Narrator	Then the angel left her.

A busy year for Gabriel. This time, instead of an old man, it is to a teenage girl that he is sent. He treats her much more carefully than he did Zechariah. Perhaps – who knows? – he had received something of a telling-off for his peevish handling of that old man. Or perhaps he just got on better with girls. At least, with Mary, he makes a better start. Instead of jumping in abruptly with his message, he begins with a greeting. In many parts of the world, a conversation just would not get going without this kind of courtesy.

As so often, the greeting is almost untranslatable. It is interesting to compare the various English versions. 'Hail' is fine for a few centuries ago; but its modern equivalent, 'Hello', clearly does not work. 'Greetings' (which seems to be the most common modern rendering) sounds far too formal. 'Rejoice' gets across an important aspect of the original word which other versions miss out. 'Peace be with you' has at least the advantage that it is a very Jewish greeting, in a very Jewish environment. It is no wonder that no one seems to have produced an acceptable modern-language version of the traditional Christian prayer 'Hail Mary full of grace'.

What actually do we mean by our various greetings?

Modern English greetings are often not much more than a friendly noise. Many African greetings are much more specific. In Tswana, for instance, the greeting 'Dumela' means virtually 'I believe in you'. 'Dumela mo Modimong' is the beginning of the Creed – I believe in God; 'Dumela Maria' is the opening phrase of 'Hail Mary'. Other South African languages are just as specific in the significance of their greetings. But the most gracious and inclusive greeting of all is surely the greeting 'Shalom', the word which we might assume would be the actual word spoken to a girl brought up in an environment of Aramaic and Hebrew. Shalom is the word of greeting, of blessing, of peace and justice, which stands for the whole of God's good will for us. In one form or another, it nourishes the soul of both Jew and Arab, and has blended into many other languages, such as Bahasa Malay, which have been influenced by Arabic. Shalom to Mary; Shalom to all who will be blessed through Mary.

Why Mary? Luke describes her with a word which can mean 'virgin' or 'girl'. She was betrothed. This indicates that she would not be younger than 12. Her betrothal would last for about a year, during which time she would be committed to her future husband but would not be regarded as his property or as his full responsibility. So she was in a kind of in-between stage, not really belonging fully to either the past or the future. Such a girl's actual marriage would usually take place in her mid-teens.

Luke does not suggest that Mary was specially good. Nazareth was not a place from which good people were likely to come. She was chosen because she was suitable for God's purpose, a provincial girl with no special qualifications or pedigree. She was chosen because God needed her, not because she was particularly distinguished.

Job was a good man, so the Old Testament story tells, who suffered the loss of everything except his life. The book of Job describes the various explanations which well-meaning people try to offer, to account for his terrible misfortunes. But none of these explanations is satisfactory, and Job goes on feeling that his sufferings are undeserved and pointless. In the end, God speaks to Job out of the whirlwind, and demonstrates repeatedly just how ignorant and powerless Job really is. Job has to confess that he has spoken out of turn and without proper knowledge, whereupon God reinstates him and makes him more wealthy than before. Perhaps we are supposed to feel that Job has simply been put in his place, and that no one ought to argue like this with God. But ordinary justice suggests that Job is really more noble and mature than God. God wins, merely by showing off and making Job feel small. That, surely, is no way to win an argument. Job is nobler than God, because he has struggled through the darkness of suffering, in a way that God has not experienced. Perhaps we can imagine God beginning to feel that his victory was, after all, a bit hollow. Perhaps God can see that Job has got something that God has not got. If God is going to grow up, he must share the human experience. So God must be born. So God starts to look around for a suitable womb.

Is this, perhaps, how Mary comes to be chosen?

However this may be, God's calling of Mary is not a reward for goodness; it is a gift. Such a gift can be scary. It is going to happen through the action of the Holy Spirit; and anyone who knows anything of the stories in the Old Testament about the Spirit of God would have good reason to be scared and puzzled. The Spirit of God leads people into all sorts of danger and stress; it changes and disturbs the material world. The Holy Spirit, in some manner which is not disclosed, will bring about Mary's pregnancy, just as, later on, the same Spirit will bring about a new community of shared wealth and common ownership. The processes are concealed, but the effects are verifiable and material. The Holy Spirit is not in business to give 'spiritual experiences' to various selected individuals. The Holy Spirit is the Spirit of God, enabling God's will to be done and God's purposes to be achieved.

The Holy Spirit is the wind of God (in many languages, one word serves to cover the meanings of 'breath', 'wind', and 'spirit'). Even in our own days, with all our meteorological equipment, predicting the wind is a hazardous enterprise; experts get it wrong. Still less can we organize it to fit our programmes. Similarly with the Wind of God. Some statements of Christian faith (such as the baptism and confirmation services of the Church of England Alternative Service Book) give the impression that the Holy Spirit's concerns are limited to the Church, in the range of things which are controlled by the clergy. Gabriel's message is that, in the first instance, the Holy Spirit is going to be at work in the pregnancy of Mary. The constant theme of the annunciations, to Zechariah and to Mary, is that there

is a new possibility. Within the depressing religious and
political situation of the people of Israel, there is a
hidden potential, represented by the unexpected pregnancy of an old woman and the unexpected pregnancy
of an unmarried girl. What is past is important; what
has been given to God's people in the past is not being
denied or overridden. Indeed, the songs that will celebrate the new work of the Holy Spirit will be composed
in the language of the past. But the Holy Spirit is the
inspirer of the new way that is coming. The Holy Spirit
will confirm what is past, but the most precious description of the Spirit's work is that the Spirit will lead us
into the truth that is ahead of us. She is the one who
detects and affirms and enables the potential that is
already there but hidden from human eyes (John 16:13).

Like Mary, we ask 'How?' Gabriel gives no detailed
answer about the mechanism of the conception of the
son of Mary. We may think that the whole story might
have made sense to a generation which was ignorant of
the results of modern research into genetics, but it cannot have meaning for us now. Well, God's communication is always limited to our capacity to receive it, in
days of old and in our day; and God, for reasons best
known to himself, did not postpone his incarnation until
the late twentieth century and the discovery of DNA
fingerprinting. Our great-grandchildren will doubtless
think that our present knowledge of human biology is
pretty incomplete. We are better placed than our first-
century ancestors to recognize how both mother and
father contribute to the genetic identity of our offspring.
But that does not necessarily mean that we are more

alert to the essential uniqueness and value of each human being, or that we are more competent in interpreting to our children the deeper motives which have drawn us into being their parents. And this is the sort of issue that this part of the story is about.

Mary gets no real answer. Gabriel in effect tells her, 'Leave it to the Spirit.' But the purpose of this message is not to emphasize something supernatural and weird; the point is that here, in the conception of Jesus, there is the coming together of God and humanity. The Word of God is being made flesh. This is a kind of language. Flesh is going to do the speaking. Our normal word-language is wide open to misunderstanding and misinterpretation. Flesh-language, body-language, is even more hazardous, even more easy to pick up wrong and to be a source of confusion. Those of us who do have word-language have to spend quite a bit of our time sorting out misunderstandings caused by facial expressions or physical gestures. Those who do not have word-language, who communicate by sign-language, may have some advantage at this point; but even they seem to experience plenty of confusion. Christians have always understood that, through the special process of the conception of Jesus, God is trying to communicate a new and unique truth. God himself is taking human form. Christ is both God and human. In Christ we see the nature of God. God is, from now on, to be recognized and identified by what we see in Jesus. That is what we understand to be the meaning of this particular piece of divine language.

Not everyone has found this language to be essential.

The authors Paul and John were profoundly convinced that in Christ there is a radical new beginning; but they make no direct reference to the tradition that Jesus was born of a virgin. Indeed, even in the Gospels of Luke and Matthew there is no record of Jesus himself being aware of this aspect of his background. It is a tradition which is treated very gently. It is never, in the New Testament, produced as a proof or a scoring-point in an argument. Jesus does not go round drawing attention to a miraculous birth. He is not exempt from human limitations. Certainly, he worked miracles; but, at the end, his life could be summed up in the remark, 'He saved others; himself he cannot save' (Matthew 27:42). Matthew and Luke both tell us the tradition that Jesus was born of a virgin. Having done so, they pay very little further attention to it.

So it has always been possible to believe in the incarnation without reference to what is called 'the Virgin Birth', and without reference to the other stories of Jesus' infancy, which we know but which Mark and Paul and John evidently did not know. But Luke and Matthew have given us these accounts of the beginning of the life of the Son of God on earth, and we have the truth of the incarnation represented to us in these cherished and very visual narratives. For most of us, this is a blessing which we would not want to miss. In these stories, we see the Word becoming flesh.

From now on, the Word of God is no longer a series of words, written or spoken. For Christians, it is strictly incorrect to say 'This is the Word of the Lord,' after the reading of the text of Scripture. Nothing less than an acted-out word should now be called 'the Word of the Lord'. We see the Word present in the feeding of the hungry, the provision of education, the construction of adequate drains. The Word continues to be made flesh, most specifically, in the sacraments. Even there, the water of baptism links us to all water-supply; the bread of the Eucharist links us to the manufacture and distribution of all bread. Those of us who write and read such things as Bible-study courses need to beware of the great danger involved in doing so – the great danger that, instead of taking part in the Word becoming flesh, we turn the flesh back into mere words. How is the Word continuing to be made flesh in the activities of your study-group?

Mary is told that her son is to take up the role of king, in succession to King David, who was King of Israel during the one short period when Israel really was an independent nation. Whatever else this may mean, it clearly is a statement about political relationships and disturbances. If such a vision came to the ears of the Roman police, Mary could be in real trouble. Later, the Church would sing of Mary's son that he was King of kings and Lord of lords; King over the Yeltsins and Lord over the Clintons: King over the political emperors and Lord over the financial bosses. During the first generations of Christianity, there were all sorts of religious clubs and organizations which the Roman Empire tolerated, seeing them as perhaps weird but harmless, of no public consequence. Christianity was persecuted because it was seen as a movement with political implications and as a political threat. The disciples of Mary's

son, the King of kings and Lord of lords, were not tolerated.

Mary is told that her child will be Son of God. One
person is to be both human and divine. Or, to use the
old language of three-letter words, Christ is both God
and man. This is impossible, says the ordinary human
mind. This is impossible, says the wise philosophy of
the world. If words mean anything, 'God' is that which
is way beyond the mess and confusion of human life,
absolutely different to the creation. But God is the maker
of the impossible possibility. For Christians, the most
powerful word in theology is neither 'God' nor 'man',
but the 'and' that we dare to insert as a link. From now
on, we see that our humanity can be where God lives.
From now on, we see that, if God is to be found at all,
he is to be found among the lowest and least significant
of human beings. This is what the doctrine called 'incarnation' is all about. This traditional doctrine, believed
simply and conservatively by ordinary Christians, has
sustained them in the struggle against injustice, oppression and cruelty. What happens in the body, in the flesh,
is of fundamental importance to our belief in God.
Christians who think that they are being bold and
modern by losing hold of this doctrine are depriving
themselves of their sharpest weapon in the struggle for
human freedom and justice. 'The more you believe in
the incarnation, the more you care about drains', said
a great nineteenth-century preacher (Scott Holland, who
wrote the hymn 'Judge eternal, throned in splendour').[1]
In a very different scene and century, John Calvin in
Geneva 'busied himself with the dustbins of the city

streets and the introduction of dentists, to bring back body to the Faith'.[2]

This all follows from God's decision to become human by means of the flesh of Mary. But Mary is not raped. She is not merely being treated as a piece of female equipment, or a lump of property. She is a sign of the justice, indeed of the courtesy, of God. Everything depends on her response. If a girl was committed to becoming the property of a husband, and she became pregnant by someone else, her punishment could be very severe indeed; it could even be the death penalty. There could be so many other options, so many good reasons for refusing. Is she going to accept the task, a task that will result logically in her being entitled 'Theotokos', Mother of God? The consent of this voiceless, voteless, Jewish teenage girl is one of the great moments of human decision-making in our world's history. Gabriel gives her a voice and a vote. Her reply to Gabriel: 'Tell God, I say yes.'

And because she says 'Yes', the name of this provincial teenager becomes the best-known name of any woman across the world.

Jesus is Son of God and Son of Mary. In him there is a new start. For people who are satisfied with the way things are, there is no need for anything like a Virgin Birth, a conception by the Holy Spirit. For those who have done well out of the present arrangements, reproduction will be sufficient; things can go on as they are. But the Son of Mary is born in a culture of divine discontent, of Jewish longing for God's intervention in the world to claim it as his own. Those who hope for real change are hoping for something as impossible as a Virgin Birth. And it can happen.

Questions for Groups

1. Look again at the first two questions from the previous unit. Do you have any further ideas of how God's initiatives have been at work?

2. Are there some specific ways in which the Word is being made flesh in your church or your area? Are there some specific ways in which you are being called to recognize God in the most unlikely places?

3. Notice the 'impossible possibilities' that have been happening in various parts of the world in the last ten years or so; do you see these as lucky accidents, or as a result of human skill, or as something to do with divine initiative and human consent . . . or what?

4. The festival of the Annunciation to the Blessed Virgin Mary (25 March) is one of the major festivals in the Church calendar. Can you work out some form of celebration or liturgy to mark this festival?

For Prayer and Reflection

Hail Mary, full of grace, the Lord is with thee. Blessed art thou among women, and blessed is the fruit of thy womb, Jesus. Holy Mary, Mother of God, pray for us sinners, now and at the hour of our death. Amen.

If this traditional Christian prayer is part of your own spiritual custom, fine. If not, find someone for whom it is home ground, and invite them to share with you its meaning and value for them.

> No wind at the window,
> no knock on the door;
> no light from the lampstand,
> no foot on the floor;
> no dream born of tiredness,
> no ghost raised by fear,
> just an angel and a woman,
> and a voice in her ear.
>
> 'Oh Mary, Oh Mary,
> don't hide from my face.
> Be glad that you're favoured
> and filled with God's grace.

The time for redeeming
the world has begun;
and you are requested
to mother God's son.

'This child must be born
that the kingdom might come:
salvation for many,
destruction for some;
both end and beginning,
both message and sign;
both victor and victim,
both yours and divine.'

No payment was promised,
no promises made;
no wedding was dated,
no blueprint displayed.
Yet Mary, consenting
to what none could guess,
replied with conviction,
'Tell God, I say yes.'[3]

3

The Visit of Mary to Elizabeth
Luke 1:39–56

Narrator	Mary got ready and hurried off to a town in the hill-country of Judaea. She went into Zechariah's house and greeted Elizabeth. When Elizabeth heard Mary's greeting, the baby moved within her. Elizabeth was filled with the Holy Spirit and said in a loud voice:
Elizabeth	You are the most blessed of all women, and blessed is the child you will bear! Why should this great thing happen to me, that my Lord's mother comes to visit me? For as soon as I heard your greeting, the baby within me jumped with gladness. How happy you are to believe that the Lord's message to you will come true!
Narrator	Mary said:
Mary	My heart praises the Lord; my soul is glad because of God my Saviour, for he has remembered me, his lowly servant! From now on all people will call me happy, because of the great things the mighty God has done for me. His name is holy; from one generation to another he shows mercy to those who honour him.

He has stretched out his mighty arm
and scattered the proud with all their plans.
He has brought down mighty kings from their
    thrones,
and lifted up the lowly.
He has filled the hungry with good things,
and sent the rich away with empty hands.
He has kept the promise he made to our
    ancestors,
and has come to the help of his servant Israel.
He has remembered to show mercy to Abraham
and to all his descendants for ever!

Narrator   Mary stayed about three months with Elizabeth
and then went back home.

Most of the writing which is called 'theology' has been written by members of that half of the human race who cannot become pregnant. What you are now reading is no exception. Luke was also a man; but he was also known as 'the beloved physician'. Perhaps that is why he had the wisdom to give us this story of the meeting of two pregnant women. He tells us of their conversation, which is the first dialogue of Christian theology. Here, more than anywhere else, those of us who are male need to switch off our microphones and listen for a change.

This is a meeting of two women with strange and unexpected pregnancies. One of them has a grievously disabled husband; the other has no husband at all. Elizabeth has been in disgrace for her failure to become pregnant. Now, no doubt, there will be chatterers who will say that she is too old to be a mother. Mary is in danger of being in disgrace for becoming pregnant without the

The Visitation

contribution of her betrothed man. No doubt the chatterers will be saying that she is too young, that she should have waited till she was properly married. Mary hurries. She loses no time in going to the one person with whom she can find support and companionship. Whatever anyone else may say, she can depend on the sisterly solidarity of another woman whose life is being steered by the sheer physicalness of what is going on inside herself.

For the most part, the Bible seems to treat pregnancy and childbirth as a process to be more or less taken for granted. But here, there is some sense of the hidden wonder of the process. At six months, in the darkness inside Elizabeth, nourished by Elizabeth, held securely by a system of muscles which soon will be pushing and expelling, this foetus is sensitive to the environment of friendship and holiness brought by newly-pregnant Mary. This kick inside Elizabeth is the first recognition of the coming of the Son of God. This is what Elizabeth makes possible. Surely a male story-writer could not have invented this dialogue! Next to the human brain, the most wonderful thing in the physical universe is the female human body. A man can only watch and marvel.

Mary is welcome. Elizabeth, as a priest's wife with a disabled husband, must be glad to have someone with whom she can at last have a proper conversation. She must contrast Mary's teenage enthusiasm with poor old Zechariah's silent scepticism.

Previously in the story, there have been promises about the Holy Spirit. But now, for the first time, we see the Holy Spirit actually in action. This elderly mother-to-be is inspired to sing the first song in praise of the incarnation of the Son of God. (Elizabeth's words to Mary are actually in verse form, just as much as the other songs which are to follow in this story; unfortunately they are not usually printed as poetry in English versions.) Christian devotion has strung together Gabriel's words and Elizabeth's words to make the prayer which starts 'Hail Mary'. It forms a celebration of God's initiative in the new creation, the presence of God on earth in the person of the one who is Son of God and Son of Mary. The incarnation would still be the incarnation if we did not have this song and this story. But a doctrine which speaks to the intellect is one thing; a story and a song which speak to the imagination are something rather different. We do need to strive for intellectual integrity, certainly. But a theology which does not inspire our imagination and stir our motives is just as untrue as a theology which short-sells on the doctrinal level. This is what incarnation means. We shall see its truth not in abstract propositions but in a community which sings its way into the struggle for the justice of God's kingdom.

That is what we are led to in the next song.

But first, let us notice another element of incarnation in this story. Everything so far is happening on the home-ground of the persons concerned. Zechariah's annunciation happens in his normal place of professional commitment, the Temple. Mary's happens at her home in Nazareth. The encounter between Mary and Elizabeth, and the more secret encounter between the unborn

John and the unborn Jesus, both take place in Elizabeth's
home in the hill-country of Judaea. No permission is
asked, no apology offered. God behaves as if he has
every right to work and act in the places which human
beings call their own. He does not have to be taken
there. He is there already.

Incarnation happens where we are. It claims our own
place. There are many programmes of Christian mission
which appear to aim at extracting people from their
own habitat and transferring them to some different
environment. Such people are taken out and given a sort
of spiritual injection, and then sent back into a scene
where, it would appear, God does not belong. This can
happen in parishes and in chapel congregations; it can
happen in Christian activities among students. It may be
useful in some ways, but it does not adequately represent
God's purpose of incarnation. Of course, there is a real
danger in the other direction, of the Christian fellowship
being so identified with a specific place or group that it
becomes merely a 'chaplaincy' – an enterprise limited
to the boundaries of the group. That also can certainly
happen in some parishes and colleges, and the church
then becomes the religious arm of the organization concerned. It may easily find itself conniving in the exclu-
siveness and the privileges and the secrecy of the group.
Our intention of being true to the incarnation can be
hijacked, almost without our realizing it. The corrective
to this is not to abandon the located group, but to work
from within to puncture its boundaries. The message of
the next song in our story should be enough to keep us
in the truth. It sings of God's purpose to claim us where

we are, but also to move us to see our place within the whole wider plan.

The first two chapters of Luke's Gospel are a series of songs linked together by prose. 'Magnificat' is one of the best-known and best-loved of these songs. We usually think of it as the song of Mary. Actually, some of the oldest texts do not give a name to the singer; and some ascribe it to Elizabeth. In some ways, it fits Elizabeth's situation better than Mary's. It builds upon Hannah's song in 1 Samuel, and Hannah was, like Elizabeth, a woman who had to wait until she was old before becoming pregnant. But unless Magnificat is Mary's song, all the songs in the story are old people's songs; so, as the texts cannot settle the matter, I prefer to stick with the tradition that this is the song of the pregnant teenager Mary.

However this may be, Magnificat is undoubtedly a woman's song. It holds together different themes that a more analytical mind would want to keep separate. Some people love the song because it is so personal, so expressive of *my* blessing, *my* sense of being affirmed. Others value the song because it is a celebration of social change, of revolution, of turning the social order upside down. Both are right. This song is indeed about reversing the way things are in the world. It is about a feast for the hungry. It builds upon the ancient Jewish vision of the justice of God's kingdom, which will be a great feast, and where those who have been deprived of nourishment will have a central place. It is about a fulfilment of the hopes of those who are longing for justice, for the overthrow of tyrannies and oppressions. It is about the redistribution of wealth. It is not just about the rich becoming generous and compassionate towards the poor; it is about the rich ceasing to accumulate wealth at the expense of the poor. It is about the abolition of this inequality. So it is a very appropriate song for the jubilee of God's people, which is about justice as well as about compassion. It is indeed a song for the Millennium, which should be a celebration of this jubilee. And all this is the work of God, who exposes all the fraudulent claims of those who set themselves up as rulers of their fellow human-beings. This is the mercy of God, for which the people of the Jews most especially looked forward in hope.

I have to admit that these comments are being written by a white man, one who is relatively secure in a relatively secure State. To catch the real bite of Magnificat, we need to take seriously the vision of people whose situation is much closer to that of the Jews in Jesus' day. For instance, what about this vision of a political prisoner in the Philippines, written some years ago at Christmas-time?

On lonely, quiet nights when one needs all the inspiring thoughts to assuage one in prison, a detainee tries to project the future scenario. One day, the empires of this country and its masters in the West, from whose thrones the poor have been subjected to a dehumanised status, will see themselves tumbling down like a deck of cards. One day, the WB-IMF, the TNCs, the international banking system, the CIA and all its local counterparts, the global military

complex and its tentacles everywhere, the dictator-
ships and their cronies, the greedy landowners and
their paid henchmen – all 'will be cast down from
their thrones'.[1]

Yes, Magnificat is a song which should be heard with
trembling and anxiety in the places of the powerful of
this world. When it is sung in a cathedral, the local
politicians should take cover!

But it is not a song of hatred, or revenge, or frustra-
tion. It is not a compensation for the way in which we
are devalued and made to feel like rubbish by the powers
of the world. Those who are attracted by the second
half of the song need to take seriously the first part.
Mary's song is inspired not by her anger or her pain
but by her sense that God has already acted to affirm
her own value. God has seen my humiliation, my lack
of status as a slave (the literal meaning of the words),
and so I see that he is on the side of the humiliated and
despised. Who indeed is more despised than a pregnant
teenage girl who cannot say who is the father? Because
Elizabeth, one sympathetic person, is willing to believe
in me, I can celebrate God's purpose to reverse all the
status-systems of the world. Whatever anyone else may
say or think about me, Elizabeth does not see me as a
problem but as a blessing. So I do not see myself as a
problem. And I do not see myself as a victim; I am not
chasing compensation or justification. God is on my
side, and on the side of people like me. My soul magni-
fies the Lord.

Our hope for true change is not based on our anger

or despair but on our sense that God does honour, trust and value us. The vision for the whole of society grows out of one person's sense of being valued. This is the spiritual structure of Magnificat. It can make a marvellous opportunity in musical terms, and some composers have creatively recognized this. To express this structure, a musical version would start with a scarcely-mature solo female voice, for the first few verses, broadening out to a full choir of all voices, as the great theme of God's purpose is developed.[2] And the song ends with an emphasis which is too often ignored in modern hymn-versions of Magnificat, namely that this purpose is to be worked out through the descendants of Abraham, the old community of which Christian singers are, at best, late arrivals.

Mary sings that God has already brought about these changes. We can see how this is true for her, individually. But was she right to sing that the proud are already put down, that the hungry are already filled? Did this seem to have happened by the time that Luke wrote the song down? Has it happened in the intervening centuries? Perhaps we can at least say that the programme has started. In the ministry of her Son, the hungry were being fed. Indeed, Luke, as a Gospel-writer, seems to have been particularly interested in this theme. He includes many meal-scenes in his story, in both the parables and the activities of Jesus.

As the Church, the Body of Mary's Son, started its life it became a community of economic sharing (Acts 2:43–47, etc.; 2 Corinthians 8 and 9; and other examples). The Word continued to become flesh in the structures of justice and compassion which the first Christian communities developed. And this happened because God had started to intervene in his world through the conception of the Son of God in the uterus of Mary. But it is only too obvious that the vision of Magnificat has not fully come true. It remains a matter of hope rather than of complete fulfilment. Magnificat remains a song of jubilee, a song of God's will and intention for his people. When we work for the correction of the disastrous imbalances in the wealth of the world, when we seek to abolish the crippling forms of unpayable debt which impoverish so many of the poorest communities of the world, we claim the vision of Magnificat as an inspiration and as a promise of the deepest truth about our afflicted human race.

Questions for Groups

1. Ask any mothers (and fathers) in the group to reflect on their experiences of being expectant parents. How far did they get real sympathy and solidarity? And how far did older children learn from observing what was happening to their parents?

2. How far can you make the singing of Magnificat a real prayer and celebration in your area? Can you see the pattern of meaning in Magnificat working out in your church or in the world around?

3. How far are you in touch with organizations such as Jubilee 2000, which are formed specifically to work for the cancellation of unpayable debts owed by the poorest countries of the world? As a result of your study-programme, could you take on some specific responsibility in this direction?

4. In the Church calendar, this story is remembered in the festival of the Visitation on 2 July. Can you work out a form of celebration or liturgy – probably incorporating the Magnificat – for this festival?

For Prayer and Reflection

• Work through the song Magnificat verse by verse, leaving time for silence or informal prayer to arise out of each stage in the song.

• Can you think of ways to make your prayer more rooted in your locality, for instance by making a programme to pray for your area, and its various enterprises, street by street?

An Advent Call to Worship

Come from your homes
With Christmas cards unwritten
With family arrangements yet to be finalized.
Come share in a celebration
Which began with the homeless, the illiterate
    and the unmarried.

Come from your places of work
With 'To-Do' lists as long as your arm
With in-trays overflowing and phone calls put
    off yet again.
Come share in a celebration
Where our work is to worship and our ceremony
    is to set us free.

Come from your communities
Where talk is of Christmas shopping
And where our children are whipped up by
    advertising frenzy.
Come share in a celebration
Where we have nothing to peddle but our
    stories of hope.

Come from your nations
Where immigrants are unwelcome
And politicians vie for your vote.

Come share in a celebration
Where the proud will be scattered and the rich
  sent away empty.

Come Holy Spirit
Come Father and Mother of new life
Come let us worship
Come let us turn our lives upside down.[3]

4

The Birth of John the Baptist
Luke 1:57–80

Narrator	The time came for Elizabeth to have her baby, and she gave birth to a son. Her neighbours and relatives heard how wonderfully good the Lord had been to her, and they all rejoiced with her.
	When the baby was a week old, they came to circumcise him, and they were going to name him Zechariah, after his father. But his mother said:
Elizabeth	No! His name is to be John.
Narrator	They said to her:
Relative	But you have no relatives with that name!
Narrator	Then they made signs to his father, asking him what name he would like the boy to have. Zechariah asked for a writing tablet and wrote:
	(Zechariah holds up a placard with the words, 'His name is John')
Narrator	How surprised they all were! At that moment Zechariah was able to speak again, and he started praising God. The neighbours were all filled with fear, and the news about these things spread through all the hill-country of Judaea.

Everyone who heard of it thought about it and asked:

Relative   What is this child going to be?

Narrator   For it was plain that the Lord's power was upon him.

John's father Zechariah was filled with the Holy Spirit, and he spoke God's message:

Zechariah   Let us praise the Lord, the God of Israel!

He has come to the help of his people and set them free.

He has provided for us a mighty Saviour,
a descendant of his servant David.

He promised through his holy prophets long ago

that he would save us from our enemies,
from the power of all those who hate us.

He said he would show mercy to our ancestors,
and remember his sacred covenant.

With a solemn oath to our ancestor Abraham
he promised to rescue us from our enemies
and allow us to serve him without fear,

so that we might be holy and righteous before him
all the days of our life.

You, my child, will be called a prophet of the Most High God.

You will go ahead of the Lord
to prepare his road for him,
to tell his people that they will be saved
by having their sins forgiven.

Our God is merciful and tender,

He will cause the bright dawn of salvation to rise on us

and to shine from heaven on all those who
live in the deep shadow of death,
to guide our steps into the path of peace.

Narrator The child grew and developed in body and
spirit. He lived in the desert until the day when
he appeared publicly to the people of Israel.

So Elizabeth's pregnancy has come to full term and she
has a safe delivery. Mary has gone home. The time has
come for relations and friends to be told the news, and
everyone is delighted.

Then the question arises of the name to be given to
the baby. The father, Zechariah, is unable to communicate with speech, and is ignored. The friends and
relations decide to take on the responsibility themselves.
In itself, there is nothing wrong or even unusual about
this. A new baby is a new arrival for the community,
and the community has an interest in it. (When each of
our three children was born, the local African congregation put their heads together to decide on a name to
give the baby, and we were glad to accept this name
along with the names that we had chosen.)

In this case, however, the aunties and uncles and other
cronies get it all wrong. They treat disabled Zechariah
as if he does not exist. They leave him on one side, even
though they know that he has gained some ability in
sign-language, and that even they themselves have
picked up some skill in this form of communication
from him. So they go ahead and decide that the baby is
to be called Zechariah. They do not even bother to
consult the mother. She has gone the work of producing

the baby; she is not supposed to have any further responsibility. But she has become a thoroughly articulate
lady, and she is not going to be sidelined. She protests
to the cronies that they are making a big mistake. Nonsense, they say, you cannot expect a woman to understand these matters. So, at last, father is brought in
from his place on the edge of the community, with the
assumption that he will show up his wife as a fool –
and with the assumption that he is deaf as well as dumb
(to this day, some people talk as if the two disabilities
automatically go together). They use sign-language to
ask the name. The name has to be spelled out. If Zechariah's answer was, 'He is to have the same name as
me,' that could perfectly well be signed. But this baby
represents a new start for the whole community. He is
not to have an ancestral name. 'John' cannot be signed;
it can only be spelled. He writes, emphatically: 'John *is*
his name.' This is the first written piece of gospel. The
writer is this elderly disabled priest.

Zechariah gets his voice back. He does not complain
or blame. He praises God. The whole story becomes
public property.

The Holy Spirit starts to work in Zechariah. The effect
of the Holy Spirit is not to give a person a fantastic
spiritual experience; it is to enable the person to see
where God is and to recognize what God is doing.
Zechariah becomes a prophet. On the far side of his
silence he becomes a singer. The gift of the Spirit is not
a private privilege for the benefit of the person receiving
the gift; it is for the benefit of the whole community,
for the enlightenment of all the world.

Zechariah the priest has to take on a new role. Instead of following a prescribed ritual, he becomes a prophet, with a new and unfamiliar text. His song is a song of liberation. God has intervened in our situation, and has set us free. Prayers have been answered; we are no longer victims of hostile powers. If the Roman police were to hear this song, the next thing for Zechariah would be a spell of darkness in the local cells. In hard fact, all that has happened is that a baby has been born. But, for this prophet, there is a new dawn. In the darkness, something has happened of which the police know nothing. In the past, there has always been hope; the community has remembered the promises, and there have always been people who, in the darkness, have refused to be totally discouraged by the lack of any signs of change. The priest knows this. It has been his job to keep before the people the reminders of God's character and purpose, God's justice and compassion, even when there has been no supporting evidence. Now, according to this song, we know that the waiting has been worthwhile. The evidence, even now, is only a new-born baby; but that is enough to make the song worth singing.

The primary headline for Zechariah's song is that the God of Israel has 'made redemption' for his people. Redemption was one of the main themes of both the law and the prophets. Redemption was what God had done for Israel, when he brought them out of Egypt, out of slavery. When they were slaves, they had no voice, no rights in the land, no power to make decisions about their work. They had no value except as producers of wealth for someone else's benefit. That was what slavery was about. It is still what slavery is about. In the exodus, God had taken a slave-community and made it a free community. This was redemption. The law, centred on the Ten Commandments, was given to a liberated people to enable them to remain liberated, to prevent them from lapsing into some new form of slavery. So redemption is about economic relations and about the rights of labour. Christians may have a wider understanding of redemption, but the basic idea is still rooted in economic experience. The Jews of Zechariah's time knew very well what it was like to be unredeemed. They were a colonized people, under the heel of a foreign power, with no outlet for their own initiative, in bondage to the foreign power for taxation and for currency. Zechariah's song claims that, though outward circumstances have not yet visibly changed, the people need no longer see themselves as victims. God has intervened.

It remains true, that, where people have no power to make decisions about their work, where almost all the wealth that they create is taken off for the benefit of a wealthier area, there is slavery; there is a situation calling for redemption. This is why those who are campaigning for the remission of the unpayable debts of the poorer areas of the world are claiming that the present arrangements of international debt amount to a new form of slavery. The words of Zechariah's song Benedictus celebrate a victory over slavery. If we sing this song, we commit ourselves to working for such a victory to come true in our own day.

Mary's Magnificat started with the individual's sense of being valued, and it then spread out to a vision of

God's purpose for the whole world. Zechariah's Benedictus moves the other way round. It starts with the
big-scale vision of God's purpose and action for the
whole people; it moves into a new mode half-way
through, with the mandate to the individual servant of
God, this new child. It moves from a statement of what
God has done, to a vision of what is in store for the
future.

Zechariah sings to his baby son, listing the responsibilities which this son is going to be undertaking. This
is a wonderful statement of the agenda of a local church;
it could be used as a check-list of the church's work. It
is to be the Lord's forerunner, a road-maker. This is
unlikely to be a tidy job; the road into the future is
always under construction (as a billboard has said,
alongside some modern roadworks in South Africa).

It is to help people to understand what makes for
their salvation, their health, their security. Their real
hope is not to be in scoring points or in crushing an
enemy into the ground, but in forgiveness. The word
translated as 'forgiveness' basically means 'release' – liberation. Its root meaning, again, is in the remission of
debt. The Gospel will be telling us that our sins will be
forgiven insofar as we remit the debts of other people.
This is the literal meaning of the petition at the heart
of that very Jewish-style prayer which we call the 'Our
Father' – remit to us our sins against yourself, Father,
as we remit (same verb) the debts of those who are
indebted to us (Luke 11:4). The whole language of forgiveness is based in economic realities. The Church is a
community of disciples which receives this prayer as a

blessing and as evidence of God's mind, and therefore as a mandate for its own ministry.

Zechariah's lullaby for his son ends with the vision of the dawn, which will bring a new hope for those who are trapped in darkness and hopelessness. The light of the new day will guide the community into peace. It will not simply give peace, as a commodity; it will guide people on to a road of discovering and working for peace. This peace is not just tranquillity, or an absence of conflict; still less is it merely a private feeling of individual contentment. That kind of 'peace' is usually just a way of becoming adjusted to the way things are. But the story of the Bible is largely a story of people who refuse to be adjusted to the way things are. The people of the Bible look more like the community that Martin Luther King used to call for, an 'International Association for the Advancement of Creative Maladjustment'. It is this kind of peace which God is offering. It is the shalom of God's kingdom; it is the true well-being for persons and for society, where God's authority both disturbs and blesses our relationships, and his justice overcomes our disabilities. That is the peace which Zechariah foresees.

How far did all this come true? Surely, Luke would not have recorded the song if it was a totally unrealized fantasy. But John's experience, as an adult, was hardly a triumphant vindication of his father's hopes. He died alone, in prison, not at all sure that he had been right or that Jesus was all that he was claimed to be. But Jesus had chosen to start with John. At a time when there were many rival voices, all claiming to have the solution to Israel's terrible situation, it was John's movement that Jesus chose to identify himself with. Among the alternatives, there were the Zealots, who blamed the Romans for all the nation's troubles, and who struggled courageously to overthrow them by violence, sabotage and guerilla tactics. There were the Essenes, who blamed modern city life, and who sought to save themselves by isolating themselves in the desert. There were the Sadducees, who believed in making the most of an aristocratic establishment position, in working to keep a foothold of power. ('Don't rock the boat' would be their motto – but, as anyone knows who has run a boat aground in a shallow waterway like the Llangollen Canal, your first remedy for getting moving again is, literally, to rock the boat.) There were the Pharisees, brave resisters to the degeneracy of the age, blaming the sinners and the decline in moral standards for the nation's plight, and determined to maintain their own purity. And amid all this, there emerged the figure of John, calling ordinary people to repentance, offering a new opportunity to ordinary people to take responsibility for their situation and not depend on finding fault with everyone else. This was the voice that made sense to Jesus.

This is why the story of John is so important, and why Luke has spent so much space in telling us about his background. John represents the most genuine tradition of Judaism. The son of a priest who behaved as a prophet, John was the answer to the Church's very natural question, 'How did our movement start?' Jesus did not start off in a vacuum. He did not create his movement out of nothing. He worked with what was already there. Further, John is the answer to the continuing question which should face the Church in every time and place, 'How do we begin?' – what do we look for as we try to get the Christian movement going in a new housing estate, a new nurses' home, a new college course? And the answer is, Look for the John figure; not someone who is skilled in blaming everyone else; not someone who wants to spread the existing established systems into a new location; not someone who wants merely to overthrow the existing order; not someone who wants to lead an escape-party. Look for someone who is already a centre of creative dissent, who represents a tradition of truth and justice but who is at odds with the system as it stands. This was what John represented. As such, he was typical of the Jewish tradition. For Jesus, he was the convention which he inherited. In attaching himself to John, and then going way beyond what John had stood for, Jesus was acting in accordance with the wonderful insight of the psychologist C. G. Jung, who insisted, 'Creative life is always on the yonder side of convention'.[1] Identify yourself with the convention, and then move beyond it. This was exactly the method of Jesus.

Luke has nothing more to tell us about the birth and background of John, except this, that John made his home in the desert. He lived off what the desert environment could provide. He lived in the place where God's people traditionally had been trained, where they could learn to depend only on the companionship of God, where there was nothing to exploit. So he learned to be alone, to survive without depending on a fan-club to applaud him, to wrestle with the fantasies which distract and threaten to manipulate the motives of even the most dedicated servants of God. So it is not surprising that, after receiving baptism at the hands of John, Jesus himself went off into the desert to learn the same disciplines. Any disciple-community which means business in its obedience to Christ will need, at some point, to move into the desert, the place where nothing happens and where God seems a mighty long way off. This can be a grim experience, an experience from which we might wish to be protected. But if a church, in its pastoral kindliness, tries to protect its members from experiencing the desert, it will have only itself to blame, if those members get stuck in a groove of immaturity and refuse to face the hard demands of discipleship. Yes, come to church – and welcome to the desert!

Questions for Groups

1. How far do people with disabilities, and with communication-difficulties, fit into your community? How far do you know about your feelings and their language? Are they left on the sidelines, so that they are people who are talked about rather than talked to?

2. Go through the last section of the Benedictus,

which starts off 'And you, child . . .' Can you use this as a checklist of your church's agenda? How far is your church a community which expresses the forgiveness of God? (People may receive the formal or sacramental word of forgiveness in church, and that is an immense blessing; but are they treated as forgiven people in the ordinary life of the congregation? Try this out on a discharged prisoner or a young person who has 'been in trouble'.) How far is your church involved in the struggle against modern forms of slavery?

3. Do you recognize, in your church's experience, people who represent the kind of contribution which John made? How do new things begin? With whom do they begin?

4. What, in your experience, as individuals or as a community, represents the experience of the desert?

5. In the Church calendar, the festival of the Birth of John the Baptist occurs on 24 June. Can you work out some special ceremony or liturgy – perhaps incorporating the Benedictus – to celebrate this festival?

6. At this point in a group's programme, it might be useful to go back over these four sections of the story, and look again at the three annunciations and songs, of Elizabeth, Mary and Zechariah. The group can

divide into three teams, one for each of these characters. Each team should identify itself with its character, and ask, 'What is happening to me? What does
it feel like? What do I look forward to?' After ten or
twelve minutes of this, one or two members from
each team can detach from their own team and go
to visit another team – Mary to Zechariah, Zechariah
to Elizabeth, Elizabeth to Mary, to compare experiences and feelings. From this, the group may be able
to get a further idea of how God works, of how
annunciations and new beginnings happen.

For Prayer and Reflection

- Work through the Benedictus as a song and a
  prayer, verse by verse, with plenty of space for
  putting in your own praise and prayer either aloud
  or silently.

- Remember disabled Zechariah, sidelined by his
  friends and neighbours. Certainly, we should pray
  for people with disabilities; but those who reckon
  themselves to be non-disabled should recognize
  that they are in one world with the disabled. The
  Church is a team of people, all of whom are incomplete; and there are things which the disabled
  know which the non-disabled do not know.

Prayers of a Disabled Church

We are people of limited speech.

You Christ are the Word of God.

Use us to speak what you wish to have spoken.

We are people with limited hearing.

You Christ are the listener who is alert to the world's cry.

Use us to hear what you wish to have heard.

We are people with limited vision.

You Christ are the light shining in darkness.

Use us to see what you wish to be seen.

We are people with limited ability to move around.

You Christ are the companion who walks with us and who also stays still with us.

Use us to be present where you wish to be present.

We are people who have difficulties in learning.

You Christ are the mind of God which grows and responds.

Use us to be learners of what you wish to be learned.

Take us as we are,
and make us what you wish us to be. Amen.

- 'The road to the future is always under construction.'

Leader: Hear again our calling:
              You will go before the Lord to prepare
                 his ways.
Response: Wait for the Lord, whose day is near;
              Wait for the Lord, keep watch, take
                 heart.[2]
Leader: You will give knowledge of salvation to
                 his people
              by the forgiveness of their sins.
Response: Wait for the Lord, whose day is near;
              Wait for the Lord, keep watch, take
                 heart.
Leader: By the tender mercy of our God
              the dawn from on high will break upon
                 us.
Response: Wait for the Lord, whose day is near;
              Wait for the Lord, keep watch, take
                 heart.
Leader: To give light to those who sit in
                 darkness
              and the shadow of death.
Response: Wait for the Lord, whose day is near;
              Wait for the Lord, keep watch, take
                 heart.
Leader: To guide our feet into the way of
                 peace.

Response: Wait for the Lord, whose day is near;
Wait for the Lord, keep watch, take
heart.

Leader: This is the promise of the Lord;

Response: His promise will be fulfilled.

5

The Birth of Jesus
Luke 2:1–20

Narrator	The Emperor Augustus ordered a census to be taken throughout the Roman Empire.
Commentator	When this first census took place, Quirinius was the governor of Syria.
Narrator	Everyone, then, went to register himself, each to his own town.
	Joseph went from the town of Nazareth in Galilee to the town of Bethlehem in Judaea, the birthplace of King David.
Commentator	Joseph went there because he was a descendant of David.
Narrator	He went to register with Mary, who was promised in marriage to him. She was pregnant, and while they were in Bethlehem, the time came for her to have her baby. She gave birth to her first son, wrapped him in strips of cloth and laid him in a manger – there was no room for them to stay in the inn.
	There were shepherds living out in the fields near Bethlehem, keeping watch over their flocks at night. An angel of the Lord appeared to them, and the glory of the Lord shone around them, and they were terrified. But the angel said to them:

Angel	Do not be afraid. I bring you good news of great joy that will be for all the people. Today in the town of David a Saviour has been born to you; he is Christ the Lord. This will be a sign to you: You will find a baby wrapped in cloths and lying in a manger.
Narrator	Suddenly a great company of the heavenly host appeared with the angel, praising God.
Chorus	Glory to God in the highest and on earth peace to all on whom his favour rests.
Narrator	When the angels had left them and gone into heaven, the shepherds said to one another:
Shepherd 1	Let's go to Bethlehem –
Shepherd 2	And see this thing that has happened –
Shepherd 3	Which the Lord has told us about.
Narrator	So they hurried off and found Mary and Joseph, and the baby, who was lying in the manger. When they had seen him, they spread the word concerning what had been told them about this child, and all who heard it were amazed at what the shepherds said to them. But Mary treasured up all these things and pondered them in her heart. The shepherds returned, glorifying and praising God for all the things they had heard and seen, which were just as they had been told.

So we come to the heart of the Christmas story. Here is the story which is the best-known and most widely celebrated birth-story in the world. Everyone knows it. We are reminded of it in carols, cards, tableaux, public holidays, political speeches, office parties. It is the basis of a huge industry. It is the end-point of a countdown of months, weeks and days – more so than ever with the approach of a new century, dated from the birth of Christ.

We need not be too snooty about all this. The straight fact is, the story has worked. God knew that human minds and wills would not be caught by words on their own, however divine and powerful. Christmas is a story. The Word has been made flesh. And this has, clearly, caught our imagination and our devotion. The Christmas culture has been a spin-off from this central thing.

But the story, like any story which gets a lot of publicity, has been bent around a good deal in the process. It often comes across as tame and boring; it gets tarted-up to look deliberately old-fashioned; instead of being an alarming surprise, it becomes rehearsed and predictable. Worst of all, at some points its meaning is reversed, so that the divine baby becomes something weird and not recognizable as human; 'little Lord Jesus, no crying he makes' is a way of putting a massive difference between this baby and any other baby. (In St Alkmund's Church, Shrewsbury, there hangs a painting of Mary and Jesus. At least, I suppose it is of Mary and Jesus; otherwise why would they hang it up in a church? There is one feature which makes me hope very much that this is the intention, a feature which distinguishes it from every other such painting that I have seen. In this picture, the infant Jesus is very obviously bawling his head off. This fits in with the story of St Francis, who threw out the doll from the crib at a Christmas service and replaced it with the crying baby of an embarrassed mother.)

We are asked to sing, 'Veiled in flesh the Godhead

see'. This suggests that Jesus is after all only God in a temporary disguise; God really remains as distant from this world as ever, and we need not bother about trying to recognize God in the insignificant human being alongside us.

With this sort of misunderstanding all around us, perhaps we can be forgiven if sometimes we wish that we could get away from Christmas, and instead think seriously about the meaning of the birth of Jesus. Let us try to see what the story is saying; let us try to see what difference this might make to the way we actually do celebrate Christmas in our churches. For this purpose, it would be a good thing to take this particular study at a time of year well away from Christmas-time.

In telling us about the conception of John, Luke pinned the date down clearly within the history of the Jewish people. Now he gives a more detailed location of the birth of Jesus as an event within the wider world of the Roman Empire. It is as if he was saying, 'This happened when Bill Clinton was President of the USA, and when the International Monetary Fund had announced new arrangements for regulating interest-rates.' The birth of Jesus is dated according to a Roman political calendar. The time will come when Rome's calendar will give way to a new calendar, dated from this apparently insignificant event in a marginal province of the Empire.

Rome's colonized peoples, such as the Jews, could complain about having their own history bent to fit Rome's dating-system. As we Christians celebrate the year which we call AD 2000, perhaps we should pause and ask what right we think we have to expect the rest of the world to dance to our tune. In our book, the arrival of this baby bisects human history, dividing BC from AD. Fine. But other communities are entitled to ask, Is this just a new empire playing power-games with the calendar? Or, have the followers of this baby made his teachings so effective that the AD world is really different, in justice and compassion, to the BC world which was there previously?

As Mr Gladstone pointed out in 1879, the Romans put their faith in the values of Freedom and Empire – Freedom for us citizens, and Empire over everyone else. That was the situation into which Jesus was born, represented by the authorities whom Luke refers to, Caesar Augustus, Emperor of Rome, and Publius Sulpicius Quirinius, Consul of Rome and Legate of Syria. Are our present world-powers, which organize everything by reference to 'AD', any more generous? Is the millennium-bug perhaps one in the eye for the 'Christian' nations, on account of their arrogance?

According to the old translations, Caesar ordered that 'all the world should be taxed'. Strictly, the new versions are correct in saying that everyone was to be enrolled. There was to be a census. But the purpose of the census was to provide the basis for the poll-tax. This is what colonization is about; it is to obtain revenue from the poor communities to send to the rich communities. The poor communities are kept in a state of permanent indebtedness. Taxation happened by order of the Emperor. Jesus and his parents and his whole nation were victims of this programme. So the older translations are not wrong, in their reference to taxation.

It is not clear which census Luke is referring to. According to other records, the big public census under Quirinius took place several years after the death of Herod; with several different dating-systems in operation, Luke may have got the dates confused. But it is still true to life, that petty bureaucracies shunt people around from place to place and from office to office. Even in a fairly benign and enfranchized society, a person may have to spend days shuffling between unemployment benefit office and housing benefit office and income support office and disability benefit office. In spite of there being a Council office in the next village, you may have to cross a mountain range to report a pothole. (The Church may give the impression of being just another bureaucracy, in the way that it deals with people who come to it for weddings and baptisms – all for the best possible reasons, of course!) When black South Africans had no vote, the Bantu Administration Department would take it as absolutely normal that a man would have to travel many miles to his so-called 'homeland' in order to register his existence.

Jesus was born in a community which had neither voice nor vote. John the Baptist was born in the security of a priestly household, surrounded by well-wishers, friends and neighbours. In Christ, God is born of parents who are shunted around by an oppressive foreign government, among people who are treated as rubbish. Our natural mind wants to associate 'God' with the top, with the highest and most beautiful sides of the world; we expect that those top people in Church and society, those who are highest, most respected, most educated, will be nearest to God and will know most about God. Incarnation says that if you want to find God you must look for him at the bottom of the pile. That is where he has chosen to be found. There are things the poor know which the rich do not know. There are things the sick know which the healthy do not know. And there are things the foolish know which the clever do not know. This is spelled out at Bethlehem.

Joseph has to obey the foreign governor's ruling in spite of the fact that Mary is at the very last stage of pregnancy. He has to face the embarrassment of chasing round a strange town while her contractions are getting stronger and stronger, looking for somewhere safe for her delivery. The only vacant place is a feeding-trough normally used by animals. This is, at least, better than the bare floor. In this trough, mounted on a bench, the baby will be safe from the hooves of the animals. Jesus is to be the one who gives his body to be bread for the world. Here he rests on the animals' dinner-plate. This is where the Son of God is born. And he is wrapped up in strips of cloth, rather like bandages. These 'swaddling-clothes' were the first and simplest clothing for a new human being, wrapped round his limbs with the intention of keeping them from getting out of shape in the first few hours of life. Kings and paupers alike start life in this way (Wisdom 7:3–6); Jesus is no exception.

Now the remarkable thing about Luke's story is that it is not told as a story of embarrassment or shame or protest. Quite the contrary; it is told as a story of wonder and grace. We are not asked to pity or complain. God has gone out of his way, not just to be incarnate but to be incarnate in this confused and messy manner. This is, surely, why the story has made its appeal, and continues to do so, in spite of all the distracting decorations and misleading songs. This is a story which makes its special claim upon children. It tells of supremely important things happening among people who have little power or status. It fits well as the beginning of the life of one who, in an unprecedented way, gave value and status to children, insisting that they were not just future adults but were in themselves representatives of the nature of God's kingdom.

So the first people who hear about this event are themselves people of no social or religious status. Shepherds are abiding in the fields. This is the strict meaning of the word which Luke uses. The field is their home; they are people of no fixed abode. Their duties mean that they have very little opportunity to take part in social or religious activities. They work anti-social hours; they have had to accept employment outside the normal timeframes which the more powerful members of society have chosen for their own convenience. In the literature of those days, herdsmen were reckoned to be people of doubtful character and unreliable honesty – along with pigeon-trainers, gamblers, and traders in sabbath-year produce. So these men are outsiders of society. They are employed to protect other people's property. They are security guards on nightshift. They are expected to be tough and vigilant, capable of coping with rogues and thieves. These are the people to whom the message comes, in the dark. Nothing in their experience has

The Shepherds

prepared them for this kind of emergency. No wonder they are scared.

There is no better exposition of the wonderful ironies of this story than the Play of the Shepherds, the *Secunda Pastorum*, in the fifteenth-century Wakefield Miracle Plays. The greater part of the play is a crazy farce about a pair of Yorkshire shepherds, Coll and Gib, and their unreliable young assistant Daw. They are out in the open on a wild night with their sheep, swapping their complaints about bosses and taxes and women and the younger generation. A traveller called Mak comes along. The three shepherds go to sleep, and Mak takes the opportunity to grab a fat ram; he hurries home to his cottage with it. His wife, Gill, is terrified that he will be caught and executed as a sheep-stealer; she decides to put the sheep in a cradle and lie down beside it, cover it with a blanket, and pretend that it is her new-born son. The three shepherds come to the cottage; they search for the sheep, but they are deceived by Gill's stratagem, and leave. Daw, however, insists on returning to give the 'baby' sixpence and kiss it. Even Daw can see that the sheep's nose has a different profile to a baby's nose. After a lot more foolery, they decide to punish Mak by giving him a thorough tossing in a sheet of canvas. After which, they are so tired that they go to sleep again. At which point, an angel appears and tells them to go to Bethlehem. The heavenly chorus sings Gloria. Coll and Gib and Daw share some uncomplimentary remarks about the angels' musical standards, then go off to Bethlehem and find the infant Jesus; they give him little presents, and Gib wraps Jesus in his cloak against the cold.

In the production of the play, the same props would be used throughout; the same shed would represent Mak and Gill's cottage and the Bethlehem stable; the same cradle would be used for the stolen sheep and for the infant Jesus, the Lamb of God. This is the kind of world that the Son of God is born into. The closer we get to the sacred, the closer we get to the profane and the worldly. The medieval actors saw this more clearly than many of us in our day. The Son of God comes sanctifying the shady and apparently ungodly sides of the world. This world, in spite of all its flaws, can be a dwelling for the divine.[1]

This calls for the next great song in Luke's story, 'Glory to God in the highest, and peace to his people on earth.' Heaven and earth are brought together. And the 'earth' is not a specially sanitized earth, already halfway to holiness, but the earth of stolen sheep and confusion in the dark.

Angels have the right and authority to sing about this new relationship between earth and heaven. Angels may seem to many people in our day to be unreal and unrelated to our world – although the authorities who decided to erect the huge statue of an angel near Gateshead must have felt that there is still potency in this old symbol. At least, the Gateshead angel is a figure that could understandably cause terror, which is more than can be said for many of our rather cosy representations of angels in church. When we go behind the traditional pictures, the fundamental meaning of an angel is that God is making a movement towards us on earth and wishes to be in communication with his human creatures. Earth is not absorbed into heaven; earth does not become heaven and cannot be mistaken for heaven; but earth becomes bound up with heaven; it henceforward bears the marks of heaven upon it, and it does not remain heavenless.

A church once put up a big banner on its outside wall at Christmas-time, quoting the first words of this song. However, the 'E' in the last word got blown away, so that the banner read, 'GLORY TO GOD IN THE HIGH ST'. They decided that this got the message across a good deal better than the original, so they left it like that; they went out to try to work out how the glory of God was to be found in the High Street and in every other street in the area.

'And peace to his people on earth.' There are, in fact, not many references to 'peace' in the Christmas story. But, at this point, 'peace' is a central element of the message. This 'peace' is announced, not to the powerful of the world, who would, as usual, understand 'peace' to mean that life with its present disorder can go on more or less without interference. Nor is it announced to people who are secure in conventional religion, who would understand 'peace' as a private interior feeling of tranquillity. But the angels' song is first heard by Judaean peasants; for such people, any 'peace' worth singing about would require pretty considerable changes in the ordering of the world. 'Peace', in the words of God's messages, is always about external relationships. It is something which can be verified, in human beings working together in trust and justice. Like 'love', 'peace' is something which makes sense only between two or more parties. It functions between real people and real groups. The peace which is God's will and God's greeting at the birth of his Son is a gift to his people as a group, as a society.

The shepherds come to Bethlehem. They glorify God because of what they hear and see. The worship commanded by the Roman Empire was the worship of the Emperor, to emphasize how far off that man was above ordinary human beings. The worship of God in Christ is to emphasize how close God has come to us. God is on the level of this baby; that is what, for us, makes God worth worshipping. This is Christian worship. The shepherds were the first Christian worshippers. We have to kneel, to get down to God's level; in the mud. No doubt the shepherds' knees were used to mud.

God is making himself part of his creation, the material world. He is found in the whole bundle of processes that are involved in making a person. So anything which devalues human beings is not merely wicked or unjust; it is blasphemy. All sorts of heresies have been devised by people who have wanted to avoid the meaning of the incarnation. There have been those who have taught that the Son of God was not really fully divine – in other words, that God himself remains cold and aloof on his heavenly throne, untouched by human experience. This is a convenient creed for those who want to keep the power-systems of the world in place as they are; God is at the top of a pyramid, and those people who are highest in the earth's systems will be closest to God. There have been others who have taught that Christ was not really human, but only 'God' in disguise on a few years' visit to earth – in other words, that heavenly realities are not really worked out on earth. We need not worry about such things as racism or poverty; our Christian fellowship is something which is true only in heaven, and does not have to be worked out in our relationships on earth. (This idea was dear to the advocates of apartheid in South Africa; it is alive and well among people who maintain that we need not work out our unity in practical terms in the Church on earth.)

Against all attempts to weaken the marvellous truth of God-made-human, traditional Christianity insists that, in the birth of Jesus, things that have hitherto been opposite or incompatible are brought together – God and human, heaven and earth, time and eternity. This is what delighted the medieval people (definitely not clergy!) who wrote plays such as the Wakefield Shepherds. We might very reasonably ask the question, who helped Mary with the birth – who was the midwife? The Gospels do not tell us; orthodox Christianity has no answer. Celtic faith replies simply, St Brigit. Brigit was an abbess in the sixth century, rather unavailable, one might think, to be at Bethlehem in the days of Herod. But Brigit (known as Ffraid in Wales) already existed before then, as a traditional mother-goddess. She, according to legend, was a serving-maid at the inn at Bethlehem, and did what she could for a couple of travelling strangers. 'Through this mother-goddess turned midwife and nurse, the Celts were able to incorporate the Christ-child into their own family and society.'[2] This is another example of incarnation, another way of responding to the vision that Christ can 'be born in us today'. 'There is ... an interaction ... between man and man, between man and nature, between man and God, in which distinction is not destroyed, but separation is overcome, in which opposites come together into one.'[3]

Questions for Groups

Local Boy Makes Good

When Christ was born on Dowlais Top
The ironworks were all on stop,
The money wasn't coming in,
But there was no room at the Half Moon Inn.

The shepherds came from Twyn y Waun
And three kings by the Merthyr and Brecon
    line,
The Star shone over the Beacon's ridge
And the angels sang by Rhymney Bridge.

When Christ turned water into stout
A lot of people were most put out
And wrote cross letters to the paper
Protesting at such a wicked caper.

When Christ fed the unemployed
The authorities were most annoyed;
He hasn't gone through the proper channels,
Said the public men on the boards and panels.

When Christ walked upon Swansea Bay
The people looked the other way
And murmured This is not at all
The sort of thing that suits Porthcawl . . .

When Christ was hanged in Cardiff jail
Good riddance said the *Western Mail*.
But, daro, weren't all their faces red
When he came to judge the quick and the
    dead.[4]

This is a poem from a provincial part of Britain, relating to conditions of the 1930s; for people at the turn of a new century, in places like Birmingham, or Carlisle, or even Caernarfon, it is about as close and as remote as Luke's story was for the people for whom he was writing. How would you work out a similar theme for your own time and place?

Could you plan something on these lines for inclusion in your own next Christmas celebrations? Bear in mind that Christmas is about a birth, a new thing. Therefore it should be a rule (shouldn't it?) that every Christmas celebration should contain something completely new, as well as the traditional elements.

If you were to plan a play or a tableau to represent the meaning of this story in our contemporary scene, what sort of people would you have to represent the role of the shepherds? (Security guards, long-distance lorry drivers, perhaps? What else?)

For Prayer and Reflection

Not all carols, by any means, are guilty of downsizing the meaning of the incarnation. In Montgomeryshire, there is the tradition of the *plygain* (pronounced plug-ine). This is a liturgy, led by laypeople, which is taken round the churches of the area during Christmastide, when Welsh carols are sung by parties, singing in turn, unaccompanied. These carols are mostly unpublished; if they are written down at all, they are in tattered black notebooks. They are often in long and complicated metres and tunes. Sam Davies, churchwarden at Llanrhaeadr-ym-Mochnant (where I was once vicar), when asked about the difference between Welsh and English carols, said, 'The Welsh carols are not just about a baby lying in straw'.[5] By this he meant that there is nothing sentimental in these carols; they are packed full of theological content, particularly with reference to Old Testament prophecies and to the doctrines concerning the incarnation.

A. M. Allchin quotes two very typical examples, in English translation:

On this day's morn, a little child, a little child,
The root of Jesse was born, a little child,
The Mighty One of Bozra,
The Lawgiver on Mount Sinai,
The Atonement won on Calvary, a little child, a
   little child,
Sucking on Mary's breast, a little child.

The living waters of Ezekiel, on Mary's knee, on
   Mary's knee,
The Daniel's true Messiah, on Mary's knee,
The wise child of Isaiah,
The promise given to Adam,
The Alpha and Omega, on Mary's knee, on
   Mary's knee,
In a stall in Bethlehem Judah, on Mary's knee.

and,

Look around us, who created these
Sun, moon, stars and the earth which smiles so
   fair?
They whirl through space, held there by his
   word
While he leans on Mary's gentle breast.

The boy who was born, a span's length at birth
Is the Son whose span measures the whole
   world,

A tiny baby on his mother's breast
And yet able to support the whole universe
  safely.[6]

This is enough to show that Christmas songs can be full and thorough celebrations of the mystery of the incarnation of the Son of God. Why not see if you can make a song, or a form of celebration, which brings these themes together?

Finally, a prayer based on phrases from a sermon by Bishop Lancelot Andrewes (1555–1626):

To thee, O Christ, O Word of the Father, we offer up our lowly praises and unfeigned hearty thanks; Who for love of our fallen race didst most wonderfully and humbly choose to be made man, as never to be unmade more; and to take our nature, as never more to lay it off; so that we might be born again by thy Spirit and restored in the image of God; to whom, one blessed Trinity, be ascribed all honour, might, majesty, and dominion, now and for ever. Amen.[7]

6

In the Temple
Luke 2:21–38

Narrator	A week later, when the time came for the baby to be circumcized, he was named Jesus – the name which the angel had given him before he had been conceived.
	The time came for Joseph and Mary to perform the ceremony of purification, as the Law of Moses commanded. So they took the child to Jerusalem to present him to the Lord, as it is written in the law of the Lord:
Lawyer	Every first-born male is to be dedicated to the Lord.
Narrator	They also went to offer a sacrifice of a pair of doves or two young pigeons, as required by the law of the Lord.
	At that time, there was a man named Simeon living in Jerusalem. He was a good, God-fearing man and was waiting for Israel to be saved. The Holy Spirit was with him and had assured him that he would not die before he had seen the Lord's promised Messiah. Led by the Spirit, Simeon went into the Temple. When the parents brought the child Jesus into the Temple to do for him what the Law required, Simeon

The Presentation

took the child in his arms and gave thanks to God:

Simeon Now, Lord, you have kept your promise,
and you may let your servant go in peace.
With my own eyes I have seen your salvation,
which you have prepared in the presence of all peoples;
A light to reveal your will to the Gentiles
and bring glory to your people Israel.

Narrator The child's father and mother were amazed at the things Simeon said about him. Simeon blessed them and said to Mary, his mother:

Simeon This child is chosen by God for the destruction and the salvation of many in Israel. He will be a sign from God which many people will speak against and so reveal their secret thoughts. And sorrow, like a sharp sword, will break your own heart.

Narrator There was a very old prophetess, a widow named Anna, daughter of Phanuel of the tribe of Asher. She had been married for only seven years, and was now eighty-four years old. She never left the Temple; day and night she worshipped God, fasting and praying. That very hour she arrived and gave thanks to God and spoke about the child to all who were waiting for God to set Jerusalem free.

When Joseph and Mary had finished doing all that was required by the law of the Lord, they returned to their home town of Nazareth in Galilee. The child Jesus grew and became strong; he was full of wisdom, and God's blessings were upon him.

The baby is taken to be circumcized. In one sense, until that physical event, he had no name. In another sense, he was a human being with a name when he was nothing but a little bundle of cells on the wall of Mary's uterus. Jesus was his name even before conception.

Jesus is a firmly Jewish name. The Son of God is not born as some sort of world-citizen, with no specific identity. He is born into a language-group and a tribe. The more privileged of the world (such as St Paul) can belong to an international community which easily crosses borders. And that is a valuable model of human membership, which has its place within Christian discipleship. The Christian movement is indeed international and cosmopolitan. The academic world, the diplomatic world, the literary world, the commercial world, all are cosmopolitan; many of us belong in this sort of world. We benefit from it, and it has much to give for the blessing of the whole human race. But the majority of human beings belong locally, in one place, in one culture, in one language-group. In these days of quick international communication it is these more local people who tend to be treated as second-class citizens. And Jesus belongs firmly within that group. He is brought into the world as a Jew, with a Jewish name, a Jewish initiation, and, perhaps, what Gentiles would call a Jewish nose. For most Christians, the Hebrew and Aramaic languages are not languages in which we would feel at home, and circumcision would not be significant. Nevertheless, Jesus is more truly, not less truly, one of us, because of his Jewishness. He belongs somewhere, just as most of us have to belong somewhere if we are to have any real identity. Judaism is Jesus' motherland; when anyone, especially any Christian, attacks or despises a Jew, simply for being Jewish, it is like a slap in the face of Jesus' mother.

'Jesus' is a specifically Jewish name, derived from the Hebrew language and no other. But now 'Jesus' is the name given by all of us to the Son of God. Every language has its word for 'God'; the different words sound immensely different. Each language and culture has its particular background for the word translated into English as 'God'. So it is difficult to recognize and understand the word for 'God' across all these barriers. But 'Jesus' sounds recognizably the same in most languages. It is, in its specificness, a sign of unity. In South Africa, with its many languages, we used to tell people that if they could recognize these two Hebrew sounds, 'Jesus' and 'Amen', they would be able to find their way around Christian liturgy. So the blessed Name of Jesus is one of the great occasions of celebration for our community all over the world. It is a sign of the casting-out of the powers of separation and division. It is a witness against the rule of those who would enforce old hatreds. It is in itself a witness to the presence of God in the world in the form of a fellow-human being.

The circumcision would normally be a festive occasion, celebrated in the midst of a family gathering. But Mary and Joseph are far from home. We are not told where the circumcision took place. But it was inevitably among strangers, in an anonymous kind of environment.

So we come to the final stories in Luke's account of

the birth of Jesus. They end where they began, in the Temple.

The Temple stood for God's claim upon the land and the people of the land, upon all places, all life, all time. It was the centre of a community's devotion to a God of justice, the creator of all things. It represented the priority of the great song, 'The earth is the Lord's and everything in it: the world and its people belong to the Lord' (Psalm 24). It was the place where people brought their offerings, representing their ability to work with the creation and to create wealth. Its liturgies served to remind all people that what we have is from God, that it is on loan from God, and that it has to be handled and shared in accordance with God's mind. In a word, the Temple stood for the principle of stewardship, not just the giving of money for religious enterprises but the responsibility for right dealing with all creation.

Luke started his Gospel with the story of two old people involved with the Temple. Now he introduces two other old members of the Temple community, Simeon and Anna. They are the quiet old people who have no special status or prestige. Their lives are passed in conscientious loitering in the environment of holiness. They are not desperately busy. They can afford to be merely part of the landscape. They are not the sort of people who moan that 'time is money', so that they cannot afford to waste it. They wait. They know that things are bad in their nation. But political or social activism is not for them; they are not lined up with any of the clamouring groups, each with its recipe for the future. They are committed to waiting for a deliverance to come from God. So they wait. They are not important enough people to be waited on. Nobody waits for them.

There is a remarkable amount of reference to waiting in the Bible, especially in the Psalms. Jesus himself puts watchfulness very high on the list of the duties of a disciple. But this is not merely a lazy or docile hanging-around – although it may sometimes look like that. This waiting is the special discipline of pregnancy. It is also the careful, creative waiting which farmers and naturalists have to practice. Think how much waiting must be involved in the making of wildlife programmes on TV!

Prayer is a willingness to wait; it is also a willingness to act and to suffer, when action and suffering are called for. But the soul which is driven by ungodly impatience will miss God's timing, and may well get badly in the way of God's purposes. In the Second Letter of Peter, there is a subtle linking of two apparently opposite disciplines; we are both to wait for and to hasten the coming of the day of the Lord (2 Peter 3:12). When we are primarily conscious of the terrible state of things in the world, this is a useful text to pin on to our hearts. Behind creative change, indeed behind the birthing of all persons and of works of art, there lies the inconspicuous discipline of waiting.

Because of their willingness to wait, Simeon and Anna see what others do not see. For other people in and around the Temple, here is just another couple with a baby, coming to fulfil the rules and customs of the Temple, acknowledging the claim of God upon human life. Traditionally, the first-born son belonged to God, to be a priest. The offering was made in recognition of that commitment. A wealthy couple would bring a lamb and a turtle-dove. Poorer people would bring two turtle-doves; but turtle-doves were summer migrants, and if they were not available, pigeons would suffice.

To all outward appearances, Mary and Joseph and Jesus are just another provincial family; whatever they may have heard from angels, from Elizabeth, or from shepherds, at this point these parents see themselves as no different to any other parents. They are under obligation to spend some of their small wealth in affirming their place within the community ruled by the Temple.

At a time when most of the official clergy have little vision, when the best they can do is to keep the religious show on the road, a patient layperson, Simeon, is steered, nudged, and authorized by the Spirit of God. He has been waiting and watching for the 'consolation' of Israel – for the time when God will intervene in the darkness and bring comfort and release to his people. Three times the text stresses how dependent he is on the Holy Spirit. By the Spirit he finds himself in the right place and at the right time. This is what the blessing of the Holy Spirit is about; it is not a matter of getting individual religious gratification; it is about being where one is called to be, and recognizing the presence of God where God chooses to be present. And that may mean a lot of waiting.

In that troubled land, some have been waiting and hoping for a king of power. Others have been waiting for a prince of wealth. Others again have hoped for a saint of holiness. Simeon's hopes have been sufficiently unspecific, so that he can recognize the future of the human race in a poor inconspicuous baby.

Simeon stands with the baby in his arms, like a priest at a baptism. He, like the other people in Luke's story who have been blessed by the Holy Spirit, has his song. Modern translations give a correct emphasis which is missing from the older English versions. The emphasis is firmly on the NOW. I have been waiting all this time. For so long, the traffic-light at this point in the roadworks has been red. I have been stationary. Now it is green. I can move. Like the rest of my community, I have been a slave, with no real identity of my own. Now I see deliverance has arrived for me – in this baby. I have a future; I can leave this spot where I have been static for so long. I have seen God's Jesus, God's salvation (in Hebrew, 'salvation' and 'Jesus' are almost the same word). And this blessing is not just for me; it is for all people. The arrival of this baby is a light not only for my people but for the nations of which we have been so afraid and which we so resent – the Gentiles. Our Roman oppressor will be affected, not by being ground into the dust but by being enlightened. And this, in turn, will mean that the shame and pain of our own people, Israel, will be turned into wonder and delight. This is another theme which will appear later in the story. We might assume that the blessing of Israel would lead to the enlightenment of the Gentile world. This was cherished as a genuine godly vision by liberal-hearted members of the Jewish community. But a stranger pattern started to appear in the ministry of Jesus. It was not that the unprivileged started to share in the blessings of the privileged, but that the privileged would find blessing in a community in which the unprivileged had already arrived (see, for instance, Luke 8:40–56). Paul had to wrestle with this process in Romans 9–11.

We acknowledge that Simeon's vision of liberation has not yet fully come true; neither has his vision that this baby will be for the glory of Israel. We, who are mostly Gentile, may indeed rejoice that Christ has come as our light. But, for most of the last 2000 years, our light has brought not glory but pain and exclusion and scorn to the people of Israel. This is not the place for a detailed account of the persecution of Jews in Christian lands over the centuries. I merely invite you, as a reader, to step back for a moment from your own history, and think of what the word 'Jew' has meant for you during your life. I think of the personal malice and the official obstruction which my parents experienced, when they gave refuge to an Austrian Jewish family just before the 1939–45 war, the terrible condition of the young man who had come out of Auschwitz, and the way the British police descended on our house and took them off for internment. I also recall how, in the RAF, every morning at colour-hoisting, the Flight-Sergeant gave the command before prayers, 'Fall out, Roman Catholics and Jews'; whatever the reason for this, it gave the impression that these two groups were people who did not really belong, whose loyalty to the flag was not to be relied on. We have not had the Holocaust in Britain; but behind the Holocaust were centuries of scorn and second-classness, which made the Holocaust tolerable to Christian conscience.

Much must happen, in the healing of wounds from before the Crusades to after the Holocaust, before the last phrase of Simeon's song can be truly justified. But, if we Gentiles can claim to have received some of the enlightenment, we are called to work to help Israel to receive the glory at last.

The pattern of Nunc Dimittis is the same as the pattern of Magnificat. First of all, I, first person singular, have been grasped by a vision of my own recognition and blessedness. I celebrate this. Then I see that this God who has recognized and blessed me brings recognition and blessing for the whole human community. To express this process, a musical version would start with a solo voice and build up to a full chorus. This is how Rachmaninoff handles this text in his Vespers. The opening passages are for a single voice; the message of enlightenment for the Gentiles is given to a powerful gathering of all voices; and the conclusion is quieter – almost a lament for the failure of the glory of Israel to be yet realized. And there are other composers who have worked creatively with this pattern, as they have with Magnificat.[1] And however the music is organized, Nunc Dimittis surely must be sung as a song of joy and release, not as a dirge of gloomy resignation!

Simeon has been acting as a prophet. Now he acts as a priest, and blesses Mary and Joseph. But, as a prophet, he has a further word for Mary. For the first time in Luke's story, we get a sign of the pain and crisis which the coming of Jesus is going to bring. Simeon sees that

Jesus is going to be expendable in a way that ecclesiastical managers and social leaders are not expendable. Jesus is going to be both blessedness and tragedy for Mary. She who has enabled the new age to come will be cut through by the conflict which the new age will cause. Jesus will not bring peace but a sword. His healing will bring division. For many, he will bring both fall and resurrection. This will be because he will have the effect of bringing into the open people's underlying motives. He will unmask the illusions which comfort the powerful and which conceal the truth from the powerless. He will represent the God to whom we pray, 'from whom no secrets are hid'.

We are not actually given a specific age for Simeon, although he clearly has been waiting for a long time. There is no doubt about the age of Anna. She is very old indeed. She is the kind of inconspicuous old woman whose presence is taken for granted, who seems to have nothing special to offer, who can be a bit of a problem, who hangs around religious places. But she is a prophetess, a kind of person who was rare but very significant in Israel's history. At a time when prophecy is not expected and for a long time has been out of fashion, she is one who has kept alive the idea that God has a living word for the present and is not just an authority from the past. She also is one of the people who have been looking forward to the liberation, or redemption, of the City of God. This was an ancient idea. Many people are content to make the best of the unsatisfactory arrangements of the present day; they do not expect any interference from God. In such circumstances, the prophet will seem to be an old-fashioned figure. Such prophets do not move with the times, because the times are moving in the wrong direction. Indeed, such prophets may well be elderly people, old enough to remember what society was like before structures of justice and compassion were weakened for the sake of giving advantage to those who already had advantage. The prophet is the one who safeguards public memory, ensuring that God's voice on behalf of the less-advantaged can be heard. So Anna, like Simeon, recognizes the presence of God in the world. She becomes a pioneer evangelist, telling people outside the Temple about the new act of God in Christ.

Anna does not challenge the powerful in the land. She speaks only to those who, like herself and Simeon, have been waiting for the 'liberation' or 'redemption' of Jerusalem. When we Christians meet a word like 'redemption', we need to beware of giving it only a narrow religious meaning. We recall the significance of 'redemption' in Zechariah's song, Benedictus. Certainly, it is a spiritual word, because it is about the action and purpose of God. But, in the mind of a writer like Luke, and in the minds of the communities of those days, both Jewish and Christian, it first of all meant a political experience, a work of God in history. God had delivered his people, first from slavery in Egypt and later from exile in Babylon. Slaves are people whose existence is entirely on behalf of an owner. They are the victims of the economic fortunes of their masters. They are bought and sold like cattle. They are commodities in the market. Redemption happens when slaves are taken out of the market, and become valued as people in their own right. This was the redemption, or liberation, or release, which had happened to the people of Israel in the past. They had been brought home from alien places. But now they are exiles in their own land. Anna's friends are looking for redemption at home, for Jerusalem itself. A new deliverance was what these quiet people were hoping for. Zechariah's song, Benedictus, and Mary's song, Magnificat, both celebrate a new redemption. Anna announces it to a wider public. If we are to make a similar proclamation of redemption to the world, it will have to mean, in realistic experience, at least as much as it did to these predecessors of ours in the faith. We need to see and testify to the release of people from the modern forms of slavery which so cripple the poorest of our world and make them exiles in their own land.

Luke tells us, in the second chapter of the Acts of the Apostles, of Peter's sermon on the Day of Pentecost. Peter quotes from Joel; the prophet had looked forward to a new gift of the Spirit of God to all people. The evidence would be that three groups of people would be inspired, would have a voice, and would have significance, three groups which were normally confined to the margins and treated as unimportant. These were the old, the young, and the slaves or unskilled workers. This, according to Peter, is being fulfilled in the event of Pentecost. Early in his Gospel, Luke has told of representatives of the same groups, all of them being found by God and being used as channels of truth. There is the girl Mary; the shepherds; and now, these two inconspicuous old folk, Simeon and Anna. It is when people like this are recognized as having a voice to be heard and a contribution to make, that we can see that the Spirit of God is at work.

The parents and child return to Nazareth. We will later have some further consideration of Nazareth. For now, we note that Mary and Joseph are able to make a home, to give to their baby some stability and security. Mary has to discover the detailed implications of her calling. There is a convent in London which has a picture of a woman hanging out a long line of nappies; underneath are the words, 'Behold the handmaid of the Lord.'

Questions for Groups

1. How does your Church receive children? There is a sense of joy and wonder when Simeon holds Jesus in his arms and says Nunc Dimittis. Can we ensure that our baptism and confirmation services are more than just a predictable routine?

2. Most churches have a large proportion of old people; but how far do they have a real voice? Many of them have skills which have been made obsolete by modern methods, and they feel unvalued. Do they have space to tell their stories? Many old people have not only old reminiscences, but genuine warnings and experiences which can enrich and inspire, if only they are given the opportunity.

3. The church is a first-class waiting-room. How far is it used? How is the discipline of waiting encouraged and taught? Could you bring in a Quaker friend as a consultant?

4. We have come to the last of Luke's songs. They all have a basis which is Jewish and a theme which is universal. Could you arrange, perhaps for your next meeting, to invite a Jewish friend to work through these songs with you, and tell you how they might fit into a modern Jewish point of view?

Church leaders, including the Pope and the Archbishop of Canterbury, have in recent years started to express some regret for the way Christians have treated Jews over the centuries. Could your group take an initiative in making this regret more local and specific? Could you, for instance, call on your Church Council or the Churches Together organization in your area to pass a formal resolution on the following lines?

We, the representatives of Churches Together in ...., wish to take this opportunity at the beginning of the Third Millennium of the Christian Era to express our deep and genuine sorrow and regret at the treatment by the Church of the Jewish people down the ages, and insofar as we can apologise for the words and actions of our predecessors, we do so, and we repudiate their actions and words. We shall do all in our power to put an end to any anti-Semitism if it may on occasion still be found within our Church fellowships.[2]

5. This story is represented in the Church calendar by the festival called Candlemas (2 February). Can you work out some special ceremony or liturgy to celebrate this festival?

For Prayer and Reflection

- Work through the Nunc Dimittis, clause by clause, as a song and a prayer, allowing plenty of time for putting in your own thoughts and prayers, aloud or silently.

- Wait.

Trash and Treasure

God,
it seems that you are in the recycling business,
  You always see what is worthy and
    redeemable,
You never discard this world.
  You always see the value of each person.

Like those that scrounge around the tip finding
  something of value,
  You sent Jesus into the world as part of your
    great saving plan.
Those who were the forgotten ones in his society
  He loved.
Those who were placed on the garbage dump
  He made new.

God,
you are the great scavenger and
the great conservationist.
  Include us in your recycling plan.
Remind us that what the world considers
nonsense, and throws out as weak and useless
  Is the most valuable of all.[3]

Christ our God,
you too were born a child
not free into our world:
subject to poverty,
harassment by foreign powers,
and dangers to your health.
In your name
let us cry freedom for your children
now, at this time,
and through all generations.[4]

Joseph
Matthew 1

The Genealogy of Christ: Matthew 1:1–17

This is the birth record of Jesus Christ, who was a descendant of David, who was a descendant of Abraham.

Abraham was the father of Isaac; Isaac was the father of Jacob; Jacob was the father of Judah and his brothers. Judah was the father of Perez and Zerah (their mother was Tamar); Perez was the father of Hezron; Hezron was the father of Ram; Ram was the father of Amminadab; Amminadab was the father of Nahshon; Nahshon was the father of Salmon; Salmon was the father of Boaz (Rahab was his mother); Boaz was the father of Obed (Ruth was his mother); Obed was the father of Jesse; Jesse was the father of King David.

David was the father of Solomon (his mother had been Uriah's wife); Solomon was the father of Rehoboam; Rehoboam was the father of Abijah; Abijah was the father of Asa; Asa was the father of Jehoshaphat; Jehoshaphat was the father of Joram; Joram was the father of Uzziah; Uzziah was the father of Jotham; Jotham was the father of Ahaz; Ahaz was the father of Hezekiah; Hezekiah was the father of Manasseh; Manasseh was the father of Amon; Amon was the father of Josiah; Josiah was the father of Jeconiah and his brothers, at the time when the people of Israel were carried away to Babylon.

After the people were carried away to Babylon: Jeconiah was the father of Shealtiel; Shealtiel was the father of Zerubbabel; Zerubbabel was the father of Abiud; Abiud was the father of Eliakim; Eliakim was the father of Azor; Azor was the father of Zadok; Zadok was the father of Achim; Achim was the father of Eliud; Eliud was the father of Eleazar; Eleazar was the father of Matthan; Matthan was the father of Jacob; Jacob was the father of Joseph, the husband of Mary, who was the mother of Jesus, called the Messiah.

So then, there were fourteen sets of fathers and sons from Abraham to David, and fourteen from David to the time when the people were carried away to Babylon, and fourteen from then to the birth of the Messiah.

Narrator	This is how the birth of Jesus Christ came about: His mother Mary was pledged to be married to Joseph, but before they came together, she was found to be with child through the Holy Spirit. Because Joseph her husband was a righteous man and did not want to expose her to public disgrace, he had in mind to divorce her quietly.
	But after he had considered this, an angel of the Lord appeared to him in a dream:
Angel	Joseph son of David, do not be afraid to take Mary home as your wife, because what is conceived in her is from the Holy Spirit. She will give birth to a son, and you are to give him the name Jesus, because he will save his people from their sins.
Narrator	All this took place to fulfil what the Lord had said through the prophet:
Prophet	The virgin will be with child and will give birth to a son, and they will call him Immanuel –
Narrator	Which means 'God with us'. When Joseph woke

up, he did what the angel of the Lord had commanded him and took Mary home as his wife.
But he had no union with her until she gave
birth to a son. And he gave him the name Jesus.

We move to a new author, with a different style and
different emphasis.

The Bible is rich in alternative versions. Some people
like to stress that the Holy Spirit inspired the original
writers. I think that we need to give equal honour to
those anonymous people, the editors. They had to decide
what to keep in and what to leave out when putting
Scripture together. They could so easily have said: 'This
version is more up-to-date than that one, so we will
scrap the older one. Or, this version does not agree in
detail with that one, so we will keep one and scrap the
other.' The editors did indeed refuse to accept all sorts
of versions of the Nativity story which people started
to write in the Second Century A D. These were fanciful
and magical stories, which weakened the vision of Jesus
Christ as truly God in the human world. But, fortunately
for us, the editors felt that Matthew's version and Luke's
version, although different, were both necessary, and
that the one did not disable the other. So the two stories
stand alongside each other, rather like Genesis 1 and
Genesis 2 stand alongside each other as two different
understandings of the mystery of God as Creator.

There are usually difficult choices to be made when
we try to represent a complex real-life scene on paper.
If it is a matter of making a town-plan of Aberystwyth,
for instance, or even a map of the British Isles, the ques-

tion of which projection to use does not really arise. But if we are wanting to portray the whole planet in the form of a flat map, we have to decide whether to represent the shape of each continent right, or to represent the relative areas in correct proportions. We have to decide whether the world is going to centre around Britain or around, perhaps, Pakistan. Whatever we do, we shall to some extent misrepresent the real thing. How much more will this be a problem, when we try to express the reality of the Word-made-flesh in the form of mere words!

Luke has been telling us of the coming of Christ into a world of quiet and poor and socially insignificant people. Most of our pictures of the Nativity story are based on Luke. We worship and praise God for this. But it is, on the whole, Luke's story which has been most sentimentalized. Matthew seems almost to be saying, 'It isn't just about angels and shepherds and beautiful songs; it's a world of cruelty, darkness, confusion and superstition that the Christ has entered. If we are going to find Christ in our day, it will have to happen in this kind of world.'

Matthew starts straight off with a list of the ancestors of Jesus. (Luke also provides a list of ancestors, at the beginning of his account of the ministry of Jesus as an adult, but a different list, with a different emphasis.) Luke has told us, with care and in the form of a lengthy story, that we cannot understand Jesus without reckoning with his background as a Jew. Matthew makes the same point by tracing Jesus' ancestry back to Abraham. He locates Jesus firmly within the history of the people of Israel, with its disasters and disappointments and hopes.

Jesus was a real human being, with a family tree. Matthew stresses that Jesus is a son of David. Even though it may be entirely accidental, we of the Davies tribe may feel a degree of affinity with this label. It rings bells with us. Joseff (in the Welsh Bible) is mab Dafydd; the Davies surname means nothing less.

For people who are secure in their individual achievements and possessions, the family tree can be an optional extra, a harmless hobby. It is certainly interesting to explore the way in which the number of one's forebears rapidly increases as one goes back through the generations; go back a dozen or so generations, and one feels related to half the population of the country – including, in my own case, some rather distinguished people and some outright rogues. Matthew's list is simpler. It is more like the plain vertical line of fathers and grandfathers that can sometimes be found on the walls of old Welsh family homes: Dafydd ap Iorwerth ap Gruffudd ap Ifan ap Morus ap Rhys ap Emlyn ap Madog ap Emrys ap . . . (with a little note towards the bottom, 'At about this time, the Creation of the World is believed to have taken place'). 'In the history of Britain and Ireland many events look very different according to where you see them from. People who have suffered history are much closer to their past than peoples who have made history, and they have a different and perhaps deeper insight into it.'[1]

To be a person, we need to know where we have come from. We need to know where we belong. This is sufficient reason for Matthew's genealogy.

But there is a strange extra element in Matthew's list.

Within his three sets of fathers, he includes five mothers. Each of them is some kind of misfit. Tamar was the mother of illegitimate twins, according to the lurid and disgraceful story in Genesis 38. Rahab was a Canaanite prostitute. Ruth was a foreigner, a member of the Moabite tribe which was a long-term enemy of Israel. The wife of Uriah was Bathsheba, whom David got for himself by arranging the death of her husband, after first committing adultery with her. A strange sequence of irregularities. And then there is Mary, and the rest of Matthew's first chapter is concerned with explaining in what sense Joseph is the father of Mary's son and in what sense he is not.

Christ is a gift to the world from God. Christ is God's new thing, God's interference, God's initiative. If Christianity is just a human invention, however beautiful, however inspiring, it is merely another voice to be added to the incessant internal arguments with which the human race has tortured itself. We believe that, in Christ, God gave the world a shove from outside itself, so that there would be henceforth a movement within the world which is not generated entirely from within. So, we are told that Mary's child was conceived through the Holy Spirit.

Joseph has to cope with the unwelcome fact that his girlfriend is pregnant and he is not responsible. The old mediaval dramatists took some delight in portraying Joseph as an embarrassed man bending people's ears in trying to find out who has been cheating him.[2] He is committed to having Mary as his wife. She is due to become his property. But this property has been fatally

damaged. It would be perfectly reasonable and acceptable for him to go public and to take action which would
lead to the death-penalty for her. But, Matthew insists,
Joseph is a just man. He does not react instinctively; he
has to think through the question of justice; he has to
work out an appropriate response. It would be unjust
to himself if he were merely to ignore the matter and
go ahead with the marriage as if nothing had happened.
At the same time, it would not be just to Mary to
publicize the matter, and to use her as a deterrent to
warn other girls. He lives with an anxious uncertainty.
Eventually, he settles on the least unsatisfactory compromise. He will not expose Mary, but he will break off
the formal betrothal in the presence of a minimum
number of witnesses; Mary will have to make the best
of a bad job and live as a lone parent. And he will have
to live with the embarrassment of a break-up which he
will refuse to explain in public, and for which, therefore,
he may expect to be blamed. Joseph takes the most
honourable option that the law can offer. The law can
provide for the formal destruction of a relationship; it
cannot reveal a new solution for the future.

On the far side of all this soul-searching in his conscious mind, Joseph is given a new way forward when
his mind is inactive, when he is asleep. The rational,
problem-solving thinking-machine is switched off. It is
now Joseph's turn to receive an annunciation.

Matthew's first two chapters are full of dreams;
Joseph, like his Old Testament namesake, is the main
dreamer. It seems that you are either the sort of person
for whom dreams are important or you are not. Perhaps

you, like many reasonably secure people, are a person for whom dreams are out on the fringes of life, or are a bit absurd, or even hardly happen at all; if so, you should not ignore the fact that for some people they are very important indeed. Even within Western culture this is clear enough in psychological and psychiatric studies. It is even clearer in some other parts of the world. Very many African priests and other Christian ministers will state that they owe their sense of vocation to dreams. Those who live close to evil and disorder need to dream. God takes a route to the heart via the subconscious mind, when all the signals received by the conscious mind are signals of devaluing or hatred or hopelessness. Martin Luther King was in an authentic tradition when he prefaced his understanding of true human relations with the claim, 'I have a dream . . .'

Joseph is a silent man. Not a single utterance is attributed to him in all the story. He is a just man, a thoughtful man, a man in a deeply worrying personal dilemma. He is also a man who, with his best wit, has decided on a course of action. Further, as we hear from another part of the gospel tradition, he is a man of practical down-to-earth skill. He is a local builder, a craftsman in wood, who knows the value both of a piece of timber and of a good reputation in the community. This is the man to whom God communicates by sending an angel to appear in a dream. Such a method of communication is not necessary for everyone. But it is necessary for Joseph.

The messenger addresses Joseph by name, and by his ancestry. As in Luke's stories, the messenger first has to address the fear which may obstruct the truth and prevent obedience. Joseph had faced the option of simply going ahead with his marriage to Mary, but had decided against it; he had been afraid of the consequences and the implications of doing so. So he is told that these are nothing to be afraid of. Then comes the information which explains the situation, and the programme for action. God is doing something new and unique, and Joseph is invited to share in it. Mary is going to bear a son. That will be her task. Joseph's task will be to accept and recognize and honour this baby, to take on the role of father by giving the baby his name. There were no tests by blood-group or DNA in those days. Paternity was decided on the word of the father. If a man gives the baby a name, that is enough to identify him as father and to acknowledge the baby as his own. So, whatever may be the situation in biological or genetic terms, Joseph is going to fulfil the role of father for Jesus. He is going to be responsible for the child's protection, for his emotional and domestic and economic security, for his education, and for his place and status as he grows up into membership of the community. That is what being a father is about, and this is what Joseph is being called to undertake.

Joseph is told the name that has to be given: Jesus. The reason for the name: he will save his people from their sins. 'Jesus' means 'God saves'. It is a name (the same as Joshua) which has a strong tradition in Israel, and summarizes their hope. It is a hope for the whole community. Jesus is not going to save individuals; he is going to save the community, the nation. He will not rescue individual persons from the general fate of the whole people; he will not detach the holy or the success-ful or the clever, and deliver them into a private heaven. He will save the people. But he is not coming to save them from the colonial powers or any other external enemy. He will come to save the people from their sins – their own sins. He will not take up a position as leader of one of the groups which seek to cure the nation's problems by blaming someone else. He will come as a new opportunity from within. His movement will be a movement of self-criticism, of repentance, of willingness to be changed by the healing power of God.

In the days of the New Testament, as in most ages and most cultures, there was no shortage of groups of people who felt that the best answer to the world's prob-lems was to detach themselves from the general mess of society. The common herd is doomed. It is trapped in ignorance, misery, poverty, despair, death. So let us find a device to save us from this general fate. Let us distin-guish ourselves by being clever, or by becoming rich, or by racial purity or ethnic cleansing. Or, if we have the opportunity, let us distinguish ourselves by being good, by moral superiority. For such a salvation to be credible, it has to be for a minority; it has to be an escape-route from the common herd. We need the majority to be failures so that we can feel successful. The message of the followers of Jesus acknowledges that this is a genuine anxiety. There is a death-like tragedy catching all people in its story. The whole human race is represented by the universal figure of Adam; and 'in Adam all die'. But Christian faith does not propose a solution by detaching a privileged few from the race of Adam. What it does

say is that God has taken a place within the race of
Adam. He has provided a new Adam. 'As in Adam all
die, even so in Christ shall all be made alive'
(1 Corinthians 15:22). And the second 'all' cannot be
narrower in its intention than the first. In Christ we can
remain truly part of the whole human race and still find
salvation. Indeed, only in community with the rest of
the human race is there any salvation to be found. If we
seek to cut ourselves off from our fellow-human beings,
we cut ourselves off from the one hope that God
provides.

Jesus saves his people from their sins. The root meaning of the Hebrew word which is translated as 'save' is
'to provide open space for people who have no space'.
'Salvation', in the history of the Hebrew people, meant
that an enslaved and landless people became free to
occupy land and to use it on trust from God. The 'sins'
of the people were their failure to recognize this God in
worship, their failure to share the wealth given by the
land as a resource for all, their compromises with other
social styles which gave wealth to the few and took the
majority back into near-slavery conditions. The promise
of the 'God-saves' name, Jesus, is that we will be saved
from the narrow boundaries into which we have trapped
ourselves. God, through Jesus, is to be the space-giver,
the one who creates room for a greater diversity than
we would consider proper. He still is the Lord of the
land, for the land is the basic stuff of creation. Human
beings may claim ownership of it, and claim to buy and
sell it as if it were just another article of commerce; but
the land still remains God's, and is for the whole human

race, not just a select minority. That was the original motive of the theme of 'salvation', and it remains in place. But we can see that there are many other ways in which people are deprived of space. By the grace of God, we shall recognize how the space-giving God is continually seeking to bring salvation, in a world which goes on finding new ways to limit and restrict and enslave God's poorest children. The sins of the people are the whole range of motives and acts and attitudes which fragment the people into rival gangs, which despoil creation by using it as a storehouse of weapons rather than as a resource to be shared. Jesus saves us by being one of us, by being indiscriminately a brother to every human being.

That sounds fine; but does it work? Does the world look any more saved than it did two millennia ago? The obvious answer is No. The process seems scarcely to have begun. Our increased knowledge appears only to enable us to be better predators on each other. But there is more than one meaning of the phrase 'his people'. Matthew has spent considerable skill and space in telling us about Jesus' ancestry, and we are right to affirm strongly that it is to the Jewish inheritance that we owe the human person of the Saviour. But, having acknowledged this, we find that as the community of Jesus developed in the early Church, racial identity ceased to be a badge or an exclusive property. Jesus established no dynasty. His 'people' quickly became, in the years after his death and resurrection, a community which crossed all boundaries and included people of all races. The 'people of Jesus' are, firstly, those who shared his racial identity. Then they are the whole human race, past, present and future. But they are also the community of disciples who know this truth and live according to its meaning. The Church is the people of Jesus who by him are being saved from their sins. The Church is a community which is constantly needing to be saved. Its sins of disunity, of censoriousness, of complacency, of accommodation to the cruelties of the world, of failure to recognize Christ where Christ has told us to look for him – these sins provide a constant supply of disorder from which we need to be saved. But at least we know something of the process and of the cost. And we will not allow our specialized understanding of the notion of the 'people of Jesus' to deflect us from the wider truth that it is the whole human race that is the people of Jesus.

The arrival of this Saviour is not a sudden response to some special emergency. It is the working out of a plan which has been in God's mind for ages. A prophet long ago had a vision of what God would do, of how God's nature would be disclosed in human history. Matthew understands this prophecy to refer to Jesus being born of a virgin. God has a long-standing purpose, and this is being fulfilled in the birth of Jesus. This provides the son of Mary with an extra name. Emmanuel is not just a further title for Jesus; it is a statement about God. God is the with-us God, not merely the above-us God. Certainly, God is holy. But his holiness does not keep him aloof from his creation, like a free balloon floating over the earth with no anchor-rope. Nor is God the kind of God who says to himself, 'Things are terribly dark and cruel in my world; I will send someone else to sort it out.' Jesus is Emmanuel, God with us, where we are.

So the Son of Mary is to have two names. He is to be 'Jesus – God Saves'. And he is to be 'Emmanuel – God with us'. Traditional orthodox Christian doctrine tells us that in Christ there are two natures in one person, the human and the divine. These names tell us that there are two natures in one God, and both are in the Son of Mary. There is the active, intervening God, who breaks into history as saviour and deliverer, the 'into-God'. And there is the patient, be-ing God, who is there all the time, working and living within his creation, growing out of the creation, becoming human from within creation, the 'in-God'. On its own, each of these names and meanings would be incomplete; together they meet our need. And if these names disclose the meaning of Christ, they should be true also of the Body of Christ, the Church. The Church, locally and across the world, represents the God who intervenes as a new and awkward voice. It also represents the God who has been there all along, who is the inner truth of the community and of the creation. The Church, as pastor and missionary, as consecrator and critic, needs to know, at any specific time and place, which of these natures of God it is called to represent. We are to be a Jesus-community and an Emmanuel-community, a community representing God's active interference and a community representing God's patient presence.

Joseph wakes up. God has taken the initiative when

Joseph was inactive. Now Joseph's sleep is followed by Joseph's activity. His uncertainty is over. He stops fussing. He immediately goes to Mary and accepts her as his pregnant bride. He gets the marriage ceremony over without delay. He establishes himself as father of the household in time to legitimize Mary's baby. He adopts Mary's baby as his own.

There is no song for Joseph. He has nothing to say for himself; his actions say it all for him.

Questions for Groups

1. How important to you is your family background and ancestry? Probably, for some it is much more important than for others. Try to recognize why it is important for people for whom it is important, and why it is not important for others. Think, then, why it is important and also unimportant as we recognize Jesus.

2. How important to you is your experience of dreams? Probably, for some it is not important at all. But, for some, it may well be important; such people, nowadays, often find that their story is not taken seriously, or is heard only in the context of some sort of therapy, which implies that they must be a bit 'abnormal'. Listen to each other with respect.

3. How do you see salvation happening in your own time and place?

4. How do you see the 'God-saves' aspect and the 'God-with-us' aspect of the Church's mission working out in your local community?

For Prayer and Reflection

- This might be a suitable time for copying Joseph's example of silence. A practical, open silence, a silence within which the unsolved puzzles are allowed to rest.

- *Christ the Worker*

(This song uses the melody and style of a popular work-song in Southern Africa, Tshotsholoza, which was given international currency by Pete Seeger as a Civil Rights song in the 1960s. Tom Colvin, of the Iona Community, wrote some English words for it, which I have adapted and extended. It lends itself to any amount of development. As with many such songs, it depends on a leader, who announces the first line of each new verse, so that verse follows verse without a break. The words can, of course, be used as a prayer without melody.)

Leader: Christ the Worker
All:
               Christ the Worker,
               Born at Bethlehem
               Born to work and die for
                    everyone.

Leader: Son of Mary
All:
               Son of Mary
               Boy of Nazareth
               Grew in wisdom as he grew
                    in skill.

Leader: Joseph's Pupil
All:
               Joseph's pupil
               Learning at his trade,
               Serving God by labour at
                    his bench.

Leader: Skilful Craftsman
All:
               Skilful craftsman,
               Working carpenter,
               Shaping every piece to fit
                    its place.

Leader: Yoke-maker
All:
               Yoke-maker
               Fashioned by his hands
               Easy yokes to make the
                    burden light.

Leader: Patient Gardener
All: Patient Gardener,
Planting out the land,
Giving every seed its
chance to grow.

Leader: Friend and Teacher
All: Friend and Teacher,
Gladly come to him,
Find in him the truth to
set us free.

Leader: Host and Servant
All: Host and Servant,
Setting out the meal,
Giving us himself in food
and drink.

Leader: Dying Master
All: Dying Master,
Using wood and nails,
Making firm and sure our
way to God.

Leader: Christ the Worker
All: Christ the Worker
God himself with us,
Teach us how to share your
work on earth.[3]

The Magi

8

The Magi
Matthew 2:1–12

Narrator	After Jesus was born in Bethlehem in Judaea, during the time of King Herod, Magi from the east came to Jerusalem and asked:
Magi	Where is the one who has been born king of the Jews? We saw his star in the east and have come to worship him.
Narrator	When King Herod heard this he was disturbed, and all Jerusalem with him. When he had called together all the people's chief priests and teachers of the law, he asked them where the Christ was to be born. They replied:
Chief priest	In Bethlehem in Judaea.
Teacher	For this is what the prophet has written:
Prophet	But you, Bethlehem, in the land of Judah, are by no means least among the rulers of Judah; for out of you will come a ruler who will be the shepherd of my people Israel.
Narrator	Then Herod called the Magi secretly and found out from them the exact time the star had appeared. He sent them to Bethlehem and said:
Herod	Go and make a careful search for the child. As soon as you find him report to me; so that I too may go and worship him.

Narrator   After they had heard the king, they went on their way, and the star they had seen in the east went ahead of them until it stopped over the place where the child was. When they saw the star they were overjoyed. On coming to the house, they saw the child with his mother Mary, and they bowed down and worshipped him. Then they opened their treasures and presented him with gifts of gold and of incense and of myrrh. And having been warned in a dream not to go back to Herod, they returned to their country by another route.

In most parts of the world, people believe that they are influenced by some kind of great forces or powers. Here are some features of these powers:

1. They are beyond any individual human control; they are objective, superhuman, impersonal.

2. They are intelligible to a small number of experts.

3. These experts have a private specialized language which they claim to understand, but which is obscure to everyone else.

4. These experts use their secret skills in order to forecast future events or probable tendencies, and to profit by this foreknowledge.

5. One of the main reasons for employing such experts is so that the employing group can outwit its rivals.

6. These forces operate to the advantage of those who can handle them, and to the disadvantage of people who are already disadvantaged.

7. These forces are believed in as a means of salvation or deliverance from other threats and powers.

8. They give most people a sense of hopelessness, of being manipulated by an impersonal capricious fate, of being victims of a system against which you cannot win.

No doubt you can think of the sort of thing that I am referring to, from within the common newspapers. The weather-forecasting profession might fit some of this description. But I do not doubt that, for most people, the element in modern culture which most fits the description is the thing called 'The Market'. Indeed, the financial news and the meteorological news sometimes seem to be mirror-images of each other.

There is nothing new about the way in which such forces are handled, or about the way in which they affect ordinary people. For communities which do not have The Market or The City to fill the role, there are other influences ready to do so.

This whole bundle of human enterprise is traditionally named witchcraft. Anyone who has lived within a culture within which traditional sorcery is practised will recognize immediately what I am referring to. But very little translation is required to see that economic forces are being thought of and handled in a similar manner.

As a non-specialist in economics, I would have been

more hesitant in making these apparently disparaging remarks if it had not been for a conversation which I happened to have with a stockbroker, at the height of one of the recent phases of turbulence in the world's money markets. This man was complaining about the irrational and mechanistic character of the very sphere which was his professional home-ground; it fell to me, as an outsider, to point out that within all this apparently capricious turmoil there were lots of intelligent human beings trying to make rational choices. That is the difference between the world of economic forces and the world of meteorological forces. The fact is, however, that it does not usually appear to be so.

At the beginning of the second chapter of his Gospel, Matthew introduces some representatives of the world of sorcery and witchcraft. Matthew tells us of these 'Magi'. The singular word in Greek is *magos*; the plural is *magoi*. The normal meaning of the word is, simply, sorcerer. There are not many magoi in the Bible; those who do appear in its pages are unsavoury characters. We meet one such figure in Acts chapter 8. He is a magos called Simon. He has impressed many with his magic and has attracted a big fan-club. Even after becoming a Christian believer he tries to purchase a commercial corner for himself in the new industry of the Holy Spirit. He gets a crushing answer from Peter; ever since, this has been seen as a deterrent for those who would try to make commercial gain out of the Christian ministry. Then there is another magos in Acts 13, a sorcerer called Elymas, at Paphos in Cyprus. He tries to obstruct the fruitful relationship that has been developing between the Apostle Paul and the local governor, Sergius Paulus. The Apostle makes no compromise with him, calling him a son of the devil, an enemy of all justice.

When Matthew introduces characters called magoi, his readers would understand him to mean folk of this kind, manipulators of people's credulity, profiteers from the handling of unseen powers. Unfortunately, the older British versions of the Bible translate the word 'magoi' (only in this chapter) as 'wise men'. (John Milton, writing fairly soon after the publication of the Authorized Version of the Bible, describes them as sorcerers and wizards, in his *Ode on the Morning of Christ's Nativity*.) The magoi in this story are practitioners of astrology. In modern Western culture, astrology is part of individual consumerism; it is about the good luck or bad luck which individuals may look forward to, in their love-life or their finances. In New Testament days, astrology was essentially political; it was about the handling and manipulation of power. Magoi of this kind were the official consultants of political leaders. They were the experts to whom the political leaders would look for guidance about the probabilities for the future. As a profession, their home-base was in Persia, where they were a priestly group within a national religion. Their craft was to watch the night-sky, and to impose a secret interpretative code upon what they saw. In biblical times, as in our own day, this kind of craft flourished. Indeed, for most of the time that stars and planets have been studied, they have been studied on the assumption that they govern or reveal the destiny of nations or persons. The study of the lights of the sky has been with a political purpose. Only in the last few hundred years has astronomy, as opposed to astrology, become something of a pure science – and in the last few decades, the heavens have become politicized once again, in the so-called conquest of space.

There is no point in us trying to identify exactly what these magoi saw, in historical astronomical terms. Their expertise was not in what they saw but in the code with which they interpreted it. This is true of all such sorcery and manipulative divination. The whole point of their trade was their privileged secret knowledge of how to read obscure signs and convert them into profitable information about the future. They worked with an in-group language, as obscure to outsiders as the methods of those who used to foretell the future by studying the entrails of birds, as secret as the forecasting techniques of modern African bone-throwers.

Astrology fitted reasonably well into the world-view of pagans, who believed in a multitude of gods and other spiritual authorities, all struggling for mastery. It was quite incompatible with the fundamental Jewish belief in one good Creator God. It is God's hand which creates and directs events in the world, and he does not hand over his authority to any inanimate object. The orthodox Jewish attitude is well represented in Isaiah 47, which is a searing exposure of the false claims, the uselessness and waste of energy, the expensive disappointments, involved in astrology and sorcery. As a servant of the true God, I cannot allow myself to believe that my future, my work, or my relationships are controlled by mindless lumps of matter far away, or by some impersonal non-responsible power called 'fate'.

The creation-story in the first chapter of Genesis makes this clear. Sun and moon and stars exist because they are made by God in the same way as everything else. Indeed, this is emphasized in a way which obviously conflicts with physical reality – the creation of sun and moon and stars takes place after the creation of vegetable life and before the creation of animal life. In one sense, this clearly cannot be true. But the point that is being made is profoundly important. The lights of heaven can be taken as the basis for the ordering of time; they cannot be given any authority beyond that. We surrender our human rights if we allow them to have greater governance. A star may be wonderful to look at, but a little child is more significant; the child can know something of the star, but the star can know nothing of the child.

Much Christian devotion has seen the whole story, including camels, as a fulfilment of visions in Psalm 72 and Isaiah 60, of foreign kings coming to worship at Jerusalem. But this is not really true to Matthew's intention. Elsewhere, he is keen on finding Old Testament references to strengthen the authority of his message; but at this point he makes no such reference at all. The journey of the magoi was something truly new, unforeseen even in Matthew's understanding of prophecy. Nonetheless, we are not wrong to see this as a story of the journeying of representatives of the powerful of the world, finding their way to the truth. It is surely a valid extension of this, when Christian tradition and art portray the magoi as members of the main race-groups of humanity, black and white and brown.[1]

So here we have these magoi, practitioners of a secret and lucrative science, finding their way to the infant Christ. They leave their power-base in the east, with the intention of getting in first with an alliance with a new political authority, of whom they have had advance warning through their specialist studies. They come to 'pay homage' (this is the translation favoured by the New English Bible and the Jerusalem Bible, and it fits the meaning of the story better than 'worship'; the word originally meant to kiss the hand towards someone, or to fall on the knee before someone). They naturally assume that they will find what they are looking for at the headquarters of the existing political authority. Like Luke, Matthew states that this happened when Herod was king. As Gentiles, they know nothing of the names and titles of Jewish kings; they simply ask for one who is to be King of the Jews. Herod is better-informed; he knows that a future king will be the Messiah. So he co-opts his religious consultants. As representatives of established religion, their job is to secure the State and to give warning of any danger of a rival power. 'Where is the Messiah to be born?' he asks. The answer is 'Bethlehem'.

Herod, political leader of Israel, makes a pact with these heathen sorcerers. But he, as we shall see, is determined to destroy the new presence of God in the world; the magoi, superstitious and corrupt though they may be, are determined to recognize the new king, wherever he is to be found.

The magoi are sent off in a new direction. They have not found the object of their search in the places of political or economic or ecclesiastical power. They come to a poor insecure household which has only just avoided being the home of a one-parent family. But their curious heathen science has not let them down. They know that their journey is over, even in such improbable surroundings. They open their treasures, their store of wealth which they have kept firmly locked when they have been in the centres of political and religious power. They have brought gifts which were designed to be impressive in a palace; these gifts have to be handed over, even if there is no convenient display-cupboard.

The gifts represent their interests. They offer gold. Now, these magoi are not miners; they have not dug the gold out of the ground themselves. The gold is the profit of their trade, the economic power that they have gained from credulous and gullible people who have employed them to practice their occult craft. The incense represents their dependence on religious symbolism in the practice of their profession, as they impress their clients with their supernatural authority. The myrrh, a spice for embalming, represents their interest in preserving the existing predictable and deterministic systems which operate to their advantage; it stands for their professional fatalism, which necessarily must resist anything fundamentally new. They hand over these symbols of their interests, surrendering them to the newly-arrived Lord of heaven and earth.

Their astrology has served them well; they have read the movements of the stars as a special secret language which no one else can follow. But they need it no longer. It has done its job, and is now obsolete. They now have a surer way of knowing the truth. God's mind has direct access to them, as it did to Joseph, through the subconscious. They go home, not by way of the political or economic or religious power-bases, but by another way.

Now this account of Matthew's story may not seem to fit very closely with some conventional preaching. But it is true to the original understanding of the story in the preaching of the early Christian communities. This is Ignatius of Antioch's interpretation: 'Magic crumbled before this star; the spells of sorcery were all broken, and superstition received its death-blow.' 'The magoi, having been carried off as booty for all manner of evil deeds, by coming and adoring Christ are shown to have gone away from that power which had taken them captive' (Justin Martyr). In other words, those who operate systems of sorcery or manipulation are themselves victims of it, and are liberated by meeting Christ.[2]

This, then, is the story which Matthew gives us as his first big story, a kind of masthead story. Luke was a Gentile, writing mainly for Gentiles; he starts his Gospel with stories which stress the importance of the Jewish identity of Christ. Matthew was a Jew, writing primarily for Jews. He starts his Gospel with a story which tells of the finding of Christ by heathen and superstitious Gentiles. This is how our movement began.

The story of the magoi is a story of recognition and deliverance. It is about the surrender of powers which hold the human spirit in captivity. In places where sorcery, in the conventional sense, is flourishing just round

the corner, this story is received with hope and delight
and thanksgiving. At the time of my first Christmas in
South Africa, I was not aware of this; but later, I came
to realize why this story had such an appeal to some of
our African members. To people for whom the supernatural world is a world of suspicion, manipulation, and
the threat of dark unpredictable forces, the Christian
altar comes as a sign of hope and deliverance. The Christian mysteries are open, non-exclusive, non-occult. They
convey a supernatural power of community, rather than
a power of insecurity and threat. The magoi are representatives of the occult and frightening type of supernatural influence; they yield to the superior power of
the infant Christ, who is giving himself for the life of
the world. This, for many, is the heart of a Gospel that
attracts and converts.

Can this be true also in places where people feel
trapped by other forms of cruel and manipulative power,
where they feel that there is no freedom for them from
the forces which make them victims and which deter-
mine their fortunes? Can, for instance, economic power
be seen to yield to the poor child who is Son of God?
Can it become the servant of moral choice, and be freed
from being seen as a capricious scourge of the already
disadvantaged?

I have already suggested that many of the classic features of witchcraft or sorcery can be detected in the
operation of the modern economic system. That is not
to say that financiers are themselves witches; but The
Market is occupying the spiritual space which has
traditionally been occupied by witchcraft. It is felt to

operate as a mindless fate, dominating and determining the lives and choices of individuals and nations. It is felt to have the power to save and heal: in South Africa, thirty years ago, we were often told that the disorder of apartheid was economic nonsense (which was quite true), and that therefore we could rely on market forces to eliminate it in due course. In other words, impersonal economic forces could be a substitute for conscience, for moral judgement and for political action.

But as well as being a source of salvation, The Market is seen as an uncontrollable fate, which blights the lives of millions. In our own country, the cost of housing bounces around, so that, at one stage, it becomes so expensive that poorer people cannot start making a home, and, at another stage, home-owners become trapped in negative equity. The cost of building-materials and of labour has not increased significantly beyond the level of inflation. What has been increasing crazily, in some areas, is the value of land. Little moral or political or fiscal restraint is put on the rise in land-values. It all feels like fate. Internationally, poor nations were encouraged to take out loans, to absorb some of the surplus petro-dollars that were washing around in the world twenty years ago. Without any consultation or consent from the debtor-nations, interest-rates increased, and now the poorest nations of the world are paying more on servicing debts than on health and education for their own people. Wealth flows to those who are in a position to make the decisions. But they would say that they themselves have no real power; they also are subject to the fate of The Market. We may try to insist, as we must, that the problem now for the rich world is not how to give more to the poor world but how to stop taking from the poor world. But even as we try to state this case, we feel that we are up against a fate which seems to have a life of its own, distinct from the control of rational minds.

One of the ways in which the money-industry has come to feel like sorcery is that it seems to have a life of its own, distinct from the values of ordinary things in 'the real world'. Peter Selby, Bishop of Worcester, tells of a revealing example of the distance between the mind of the financial expert and the mind of ordinary people:

> At a meeting held to enable people to consider the implications of the loss by the Church Commissioners of some £800 million through unsuccessful investment in property, those present were given a careful explanation of the course of events that had led up to the loss. The explanation sounded clear and coherent enough, until someone in the audience, with what was almost a note of apology for asking a foolish question, asked, 'If they have lost £800 million, who's got it?' Carefully, the answer was explained: it was not like that; it was as if a house you owned and thought worth a certain sum turned out to be worth several thousand pounds less. You were poorer, but nobody else actually had the money. This prompted me to raise the question, 'Suppose instead of losing that money they had gained it; first of all, we wouldn't be holding this meeting because we wouldn't be

worried about it; but secondly, would we think of asking the question, "If they've gained the money, who's lost it?".[3]

I am not trying to suggest that the finance industry is the only modern form of witchcraft, not by any means. But the parallels and implications are sufficiently close for us to look at it in this light with some seriousness. For some people, this suggested set of connections may feel true. Other people may well have other experiences which suggest different connections. Certainly, for many people, racism has the character of a system of witchcraft. For other people, it might be the class system, or the education system, or the social security system. Others will feel that organized religion has the same character and effect. These all come across as closed, self-contained and self-justifying systems. They tell you who you are, where you fit in, where your future lies. They appeal to people who have a passion to control other people. And against them, you cannot win. This is what it feels like to be on the receiving end of sorcery. In one way or another, millions of people in our own world feel that they are victims of this sort of conspiracy. What is the form in which it affects you, in your own experience? Matthew's story tells us that we are no longer merely victims, that the systems of oppression have met and acknowledged their Lord, in the person of the baby at Bethlehem.

To return to the sorcerers in Matthew's story: we have noted that these magoi stand for something which the Bible as a whole reckons to be dark and evil. But

Matthew does not highlight this. The system which they serve is corrupt and incompatible with belief in the one true God, the Creator and liberator of his people. But the individual practitioners are not themselves condemned. The simple fact is that they got there. They come to Christ before the holy and the respectable. They worship and acknowledge the new-born Son of God. We who come to him in worship are in a procession led by these sinister but persistent characters. When, later in history, Persian invaders were about to destroy the Basilica of the Nativity in Bethlehem, they paused when they saw a picture of the magoi over the entrance. They paused, and they spared the building, because they saw that the magoi were dressed in Persian robes.

This story is traditionally the event which is celebrated in the festival of the Epiphany. Epiphany is usually seen as a great missionary celebration. That is indeed what it is. But it is not about our duty to go to convert others, or to influence them towards membership of the Church. There are other celebrations which properly serve that theme. This story is about how enquirers or seekers are received by Christ. Before jumping to correct errors, the Gospel allows people to fumble and find their way by whatever light they have. This is not a story of human achievement. It is about God's presence. It is about Emmanuel, God with us. For God is not far off, accessible only to the holy and the virtuous. God is there to be found by those who are willing to recognize him. God adapts himself to those whom he calls. He speaks to the magoi in their language; he uses their minds, as they put their own interpretation on the movements of stars. To fishermen, he will communicate by means of fish. To the Apostle Paul, who was not unfamiliar with the experience of being a defendant in a law court, he will communicate in the language of the law. Improbable people find God in the improbable places where he has chosen to be found. The magoi were not put off by the strange environment in which the Most Holy was lying. In our mission, we shall certainly find some things which are incompatible with obedience to the true God. But, as this whole chapter of Matthew's Gospel shows, the worst and most destructive things are found in the places which are supposed to be dedicated to true belief. Gentiles find what Israel's leader tries to destroy. But, after his interview with the magoi, Herod is no longer called 'King'. His informed eye is less clear than the deformed eye of the pagan.

There are two main ways in which religious people assess the world around. One says that life in this world is essentially bad, and that we can achieve truth and holiness only by escaping out of it. The other says that life in this world is essentially good, and that if God is to be found anywhere he is to be found in it. A great deal of Christian devotion has, perhaps without realizing it, assumed the first interpretation. It is an honourable view, which has inspired much courage and self-discipline. But Christians who take the incarnation of the Son of God seriously must insist that the second interpretation is more true. That is not to say that all is well. Indeed, we will be most effectively inspired to take up the struggle against the powers of darkness if we believe that they have no final right to tell us who is in charge. God has declared that this world, with all its crucifying propensities, is still a valid dwelling-place for himself. Human beings may come out with some weird and sometimes destructive ideas, but the Christian disciple will be on the lookout for ways in which these ideas can lead towards the truth, and perhaps even be baptized.

G. K. Chesterton caught the hope and the skill of this sort of judgement, in the words which he put into the mouth of King Alfred, defying the mighty but tired lords of paganism.

> Therefore your end is on you,
>   Is on you and your kings,
> Not for a fire on Ely fen,
> Not that your gods are nine or ten,
> But because it is only Christian men
>   Guard even heathen things.
>
> For our God hath blessed creation,
>   Calling it good. I know
> What spirit with whom ye blindly band
> Hath blessed destruction with his hand;
> Yet by God's death the stars shall stand
>   And the small apples grow.[4]

The magoi offer representative gifts, the products of creation. These gifts are not just natural, like the apples and marrows offered at a Harvest Festival. They are industrial products. All have been through some extractive or manufacturing process. They represent human interference in the natural order. They represent a wide range of human work, of production, of transport, of commerce and exchange. This is all part of creation; our task is to recognize that it is all still part of God's world, that the earth is the Lord's and all that is in it. These gifts lead on to the Christian offering, the bread and wine which earth has given and human hands have made. If this be so, it is all the more grievous when the things of creation, including the things on which human skill and inventiveness have been exercised, are used to reinforce inequalities between people and to keep some in poverty and slavery. At the Christian altar, we are bold to offer impure and tainted goods. No bread can be free from the ambiguous processes of buying and selling. No wine can be free from links with abuse and degradation. In offering such products, we are alongside these magoi, with their very dubious gifts. Messy though they are, they can adorn the cradle of the Son of God.

Questions for Groups

1. If there are six or more people in your group, divide into three teams. Work out what sort of people do you think might represent the magoi in our present-day society; one team should consider who might represent the ones who offer gold, one those who offer incense, one those who offer myrrh. Then, what actual products from today's world could

represent these gifts? After you have had time to work on these questions, each team should send one person to visit one other team, to compare notes and to offer their ideas to each other. Be constructively critical of each other. (One of my favourite Christmas cards shows three solid gentlemen carrying briefcases; the caption reads, '. . . there came three double-glazing salesmen from the East.' I think that Matthew would see the point.)

If you were going to make a play or tableau to represent the meaning of this story for today, how would you do it? What suggestions do you have for your local church's celebration of Epiphany next year?

2. The comments about economic powers in this chapter are offered not as incontrovertible truth but as an attempt to suggest how the implications of Matthew's story could be translated into our own day. Try to get someone who knows economic systems from the inside to comment critically. And what other manifestations of sorcery do you recognize in our present world, and how might they be brought under the authority of Christ?

For Prayer and Reflection

Carol of the Epiphany

Voice A. 1. I sought him dressed in finest
    clothes,
  where money talks and status
    grows;
  but power and wealth he never
    chose:
  it seemed he lived in poverty.

Voice B. 2. I sought him in the safest place,
  remote from crime or cheap disgrace;
  but safety never knew his face:
  it seemed he lived in jeopardy.

Voice C. 3. I sought him where the spotlights
    glare,
  where crowds collect and critics
    stare;
  but no one knew his presence there:
  it seemed he lived in obscurity.

Voice A. 4. Then, in the streets, we heard the
    word
  which seemed, for all the world,
    absurd:

that those who could no gifts afford
were entertaining Christ the Lord.

All   5. AND SO, DISTINCT FROM
Voices.   ALL WE'D PLANNED,
                 AMONG THE POOREST OF
                 THE LAND,
                 WE DID WHAT FEW MIGHT
                 UNDERSTAND
                 WE TOUCHED GOD IN A
                 BABY'S HAND.[5]

Your nativity, O Christ our God, has shed a light of understanding upon the world. Through it, those who had been star-worshippers learned through a star to worship you, the Sun of Truth, and to recognize in you the one who rises in the East and comes from on high.[6]

The Flight into Egypt

9

Dreams and Journeys
Matthew 2:13–23

Narrator	When the Magi had gone, an angel of the Lord appeared to Joseph in a dream:
Angel	Get up. Take the child and his mother and escape to Egypt. Stay there until I tell you, for Herod is going to search for the child to kill him.
Narrator	So he got up, took the child and his mother by night and left for Egypt, where he stayed until the death of Herod. And so was fulfilled what the Lord had said through the prophet:
Prophet	Out of Egypt I called my son.
Narrator	When Herod realized that he had been outwitted by the Magi, he was furious, and he gave orders to kill all the boys in Bethlehem and its vicinity who were two years old and under, in accordance with the time he had learned from the Magi. Then what was said through the prophet Jeremiah was fulfilled:
Jeremiah	A voice is heard in Ramah, weeping and great mourning, Rachel weeping for her children and refusing to be comforted, because they are no more.

Narrator	After Herod died, an angel of the Lord appeared in a dream to Joseph in Egypt:
Angel	Get up, take the child and his mother, and go back to the land of Israel, because those who tried to kill the child are dead.
Narrator	So Joseph got up, took the child and his mother, and went back to Israel.
	But when Joseph heard that Archelaus had succeeded his father Herod as king of Judaea, he was afraid to go there. He was given more instructions in a dream, so he went to the province of Galilee and made his home in a town named Nazareth. And so what the prophets had said came true:
Prophet	He will be called a Nazarene.

More dreams for Joseph. Twice there is the clear instruction: 'Get up. Take the child and his mother and . . .' And without hesitation, Joseph does what he is told.

Joseph is revealed as a man in whom the subconscious is uncluttered and unobstructed. It is a fluent channel for God's word. I know that I cannot recall ever having had a dream anything like as clear as these dreams of Joseph. My dreams are confused, arbitrary, full of random characters thrown together in a muddle. But this is all part of what it is to be me. But even I can acknowledge that, given time, truth and good sense can sometimes emerge through the subconscious. Or, more simply, we can often find a way through by 'sleeping on it'. Truth can be allowed to move, when the conscious mind is not interfering. So I need not feel totally disabled by Joseph's evident openness to divine influence. I shall never be as easily guided as Joseph; but I still belong in the same human fabric.

Joseph must have been specially able to wait and not be hassled. The movement of truth through the subconscious, whether by dreams or by other means, cannot be speeded up by being anxious. But, once the message has got through to him, Joseph moves without delay. He gets up immediately, and sets off through the night to find a place of safety.

Matthew's story is taking us into a scene of darkness, insecurity, cruelty and destruction. By the action of a Jewish government, Jesus is dispossessed of his place within the land of his birth – an experience which many Palestinians will feel to be their experience. Joseph must have felt that it was all a long way away from the promise that the baby would be a saviour. Here we have the baby himself having to be saved. He is lucky to be able to escape with his life. He is taken into Egypt, the country from which the people of Israel had, long ago, been saved. The country which had been the oppressive slave-owner now becomes a refuge. Africa, the homeland now of so many refugees and migrant workers and nomads, becomes a reception-area for the Son of God.

So the Saviour of the world becomes a refugee in Egypt. Although it is the old enemy, Egypt is a neighbour-country to Israel. Like most refugees in modern Africa, Jesus the refugee finds a place to stay in a nearby area and accepts that area's hospitality. The border is not effectively policed. From the evidence of Matthew's account, Joseph is not subjected to immigration restrictions; he does not have to prove that he is a genuine asylum-seeker, or that his fear of persecution is bogus.

Nonetheless, being a refugee, even in a relatively benign country, is one of the most miserable experiences for a family. If I may be personal again, when the government of South Africa made it impossible for my family and me to continue in that country, we had six months in Britain without home or employment; for me, this was far more of a misery and a worry than anything we had experienced at the ungentle hands of the South African Police. Joseph, as a competent builder and woodworker, no doubt was in a position to sell his skills in the Egyptian market; but jobs would probably go first to the locals. Matthew tells us nothing about such problems; nor does he suggest that the gifts of the magoi might have come in remarkably handy in a financial emergency. But he does stress that the flight into Egypt, and the family's sojourn there, were the fulfilment of a declaration by God through an earlier prophet.

Matthew is especially keen to point out when something is happening in fulfilment of prophecy. Sometimes this may look a bit forced, and we might not find his idea of fulfilment particularly convincing. And in many cases he is linking prophecies to events which are at first sight ungodly, incompatible with any sense of divine rule. In effect he is saying: In these events it may look as if God has been dethroned, that his will is thwarted, that his intentions are defeated. But in fact, God is still in charge. Even in what may seem to be a disastrous emergency, his intentions are being worked out; and the prophets of long ago could see that this sort of thing was going to happen – even if they could not know the details. God can work through the changes that are caused by human perversity and sin. Because he is the Creator God, he is the improviser; he is always working with the new and discouraging situation which is facing us. He is the God of the Second Chance; he is not finally beaten by either open opposition or bad luck.

Only if God is the God of the Alternative Plan can he, or we, work with the world as in fact we find it. It is a common experience of, for instance, Christian missionaries, that everything is working out the way they have planned; they are confident of their own sense of vocation; the Church is clear where they should be going to serve; their family and friends are fully support-ive. Then comes the news that they cannot get a visa. Everything seems to fall apart. It can be very difficult for them to come to terms with one simple fact: we are in a world where God's will often is not done. And, if that was not the case, there would not be much point in missionaries. But God is the God of the Alternative Plan. And the Alternative Plan may well involve becom-ing a refugee; or, being crucified.

So Joseph and Mary and Jesus are refugees in Egypt. The Son of God knows this experience from inside. He knows what it is to be an exile.

Most people on the face of the earth know what it is like to be pushed around, to be on the receiving end of the systems of control and domination. There is a gap between their experience and the experience of the more powerful people who organize society, and who become educators and writers, including writers of religious books. But it is particularly for that hidden majority of people that the character of God as refugee should be most important. It should never be too far from our preaching and devotion.

At the upper end of the valley of the Tanat in Mid-Wales, with only a couple of houses and a farm nearby, stands the ancient pilgrimage church of Pennant Melangell. Melangell was an Irish lady who, at the end of the sixth century AD, fled to Wales to avoid being forced into an arranged marriage. She became a hermit in this isolated spot. In 604, a powerful landowner was hunting in the valley, and his hounds started to pursue a hare. This hare ran up to Melangell and took refuge in the hem of her long dress. The hounds refused to obey the huntsman's commands, and backed away. The huntsman was so surprised at this that he made a present of that area of the valley to Melangell, to be a place of refuge for fugitives, both human and animal. From that day to this, hares are not hunted in that part of the Tanat Valley. The pilgrimage church grew up around the site; the shrine of Melangell remains as a unique structure of its type; and medieval carvings of the saint and the hare are still in the church. Now, this sort of story would have an easy appeal to the sentiments of late nineteenth-century romantics and urban twentieth-century animal-lovers. The more remarkable thing is that it clearly made a great deal of sense to the hard-headed and unsentimental medieval people. They saw and treasured, in this story, the sign that God is on the side of the refugee and the fugitive, and that those who control the use of the land do not have the last word.

So, for them, a pilgrimage to Melangell's shrine was accounted as a devotion of very high value. (When I was parish priest in the upper Tanat Valley, fourteen years ago, the church was one of seven in my care. It was still a place of pilgrimage, but had become somewhat shabby. Since then, the church and shrine have been marvellously restored. Not only are the physical structures in good order, but a profoundly valuable ministry of counselling and healing has grown up, which is firmly in the orthodox and practical tradition which Melangell represents. It is a unique place of pilgrimage in its own right, at the end of the twentieth century.)

The figure of Christ the Refugee is one of the guiding signs for the Church's obedience. When the Church started to have some secular power, and to be itself a landowner, its buildings became recognized as places of refuge. The right of sanctuary was, for centuries, part of the custom of Britain, and was regulated in the law of Church and State. A fugitive could take refuge in church, not indefinitely, but long enough for the case to be sorted out and innocence or guilt to be established. Although the official law has not been in force for over 250 years, the idea has remained in the public mind. In recent years, this right of sanctuary has been claimed on behalf of asylum-seekers, who have been afforded sanctuary in churches when threatened with deportation. The publicity, the debate, and the cautiousness of police and magistrates in taking action to evict, have shown that the idea of the right of sanctuary still has some vigour in our secular culture. The story of the Holy Family as asylum-seekers in Egypt warns us to guard against legalism and stinginess. Matthew's Gospel depicts a Christ who shares this experience of humiliation.

But worst, much worse, is to come.

Matthew does not conceal from us the fact that the Son of God is born into a world where things go wrong, not just by accident or casual error, but by viciousness, violence, and cruelty. We are right to be disgusted and scared by the depravity in the behaviour of some conspicuous individuals, for we realize that they might easily be us. But this story is about the institutionalized, legalized violence of the State. Herod is the legitimate ruler, authorized by Rome, tolerated by his own nation. The old man, nearing his own death, is scared of a young baby. The new is the ruinous threat to the old. The new must be destroyed. There can be no security otherwise. For Herod, this is just a new twist to his own sad story. He has already killed three of his own sons in order to keep hold of his position of political leadership. His troubles are his people's troubles; that is what political leadership is all about. So the death of hundreds of his nation's children is no great novelty. He presumably feels that he has no option; he could even say, 'the evil that I would not, that I do.'

The old man Abraham felt called to sacrifice his young son Isaac. He drew the knife, but an angel prevented him from killing. Wilfred Owen, poet of the 1914–18 war, told the same story, but ended with Abraham refusing the Angel's message.

But the old man would not so, but slew his son,
and half the seed of Europe, one by one.[1]

Those who give the orders that send people to their deaths are usually aged fifty-plus. Those that are sent are mostly under thirty.

Hundreds of mothers are bereaved of their children, but Mary's child is spared. Their children are killed instead of hers. If she had stayed in Bethlehem, it would have been a tragedy for her; but all those other mothers would have been able to bring up their children in safety. In a cruel and vicious world, they pay a price which Mary can wait for thirty more years to pay. Eventually she also will see her son put to death at the hands of a ruthless regime which cannot cope with the new kingdom that God is offering to the world.

Matthew quotes one of the great poems of lamentation from the Hebrew scriptures, in Jeremiah 31. The prophet compares God to a mother inconsolably mourning the death of her children. Jeremiah goes on to assure the mother that there is real hope for the mother, because her children will return. But Matthew does not quote this part. As far as he is concerned, the death of the children in Bethlehem is simply a matter for grief. He does not have a neat solution. He knows that some of the most powerful psalms are songs of lament, for the people of God are placed in a harsh and cruel world. There may be an answer, but it is not an answer which can simply be read off the page. This lamentation is of the same stuff as the central lamentation in Matthew's story, where the adult Son of God calls out, 'My God, my God, why have you forsaken me?' (Matthew 27:46). God is not there, he has forsaken the one who is speaking. But God is there, he can be spoken to. The fact that

God has forsaken is a total tragedy, for which there can
be no explanation. But there can be an explanation,
because this is what the 'why' is asking for. These con-
tradictions are at the heart of the biblical pattern of
lamentation. It is not just that terrible things happen,
but there seems to be no acceptable reason for them
happening. Yet there is a reason, hidden within the darkness of God's way of working in his world.

The time of the Great Terror passes. The death of the
death-maker is good news. Another message for Joseph:
Get up again and take the child and his mother, this
time to Israel. So, again, silent Joseph immediately packs
up and goes to Israel. But Archelaus is a chip off the
old block. As a king, he is no less of a tyrant than his
father. Bethlehem is no safe haven for the family. So
there is a final dream for Joseph; he takes the family to
Galilee.

Again, Matthew sees the choice of Galilee, and
specifically of Nazareth, as a fulfilment of prophecy –
although it is impossible to pin down exactly which
prophecy he is referring to. And again, the prophecy is
brought in to give background to something that sounds
odd and incompatible with the presence of God in the
world. Galilee, for Matthew, is scarcely Israel. It is 'Galilee of the Gentiles' (Matthew 4:15). It is the place of
confusion, of paganism, of uncleanness, of betrayal, of
demons, of disorder. It is an area of storms, of political
intrigue, of foreign interference, of frontiers which constantly have to be crossed, an area where some Jews
have sold out to the colonial power and have become
toll-collectors, and others have given up their family life

and have taken to the hills as brigands. It is a place despised by the respectable citizens of Judaea and Jerusalem, who are quick to detect the northern Galilean accent. This is the area which, for most of the rest of his life on earth, is to be the home of the incarnate Son of God.

And, within Galilee, one of the most insignificant places is Nazareth. There are some thriving cities in Galilee, especially Sepphoris and Tiberias. But in the Gospel story there is not a single reference to these important places. Nazareth is so unimportant that it does not even feature in the list of villages recorded by the historian Josephus. It is a 'no-place'. Its inhabitants are 'no-people'.

Matthew's story is one way that the first Christians had of dealing with an awkward question. As was clear in the answer of the chief priests and scribes to the magoi, the expectation was that Christ, as Son of David, should come from David's city, Bethlehem. But, in fact, it was widely known that he actually was a Galilean, from Nazareth. How come? Different traditions provide different answers. Matthew's answer was that Jesus' birth actually took place in Bethlehem; but, due to a whole series of anxieties caused by the political insecurity of the times, his upbringing took place in Nazareth, and therefore it was from Nazareth that he came in his adult life.

Matthew is stressing that this happened not because of a whole lot of unfortunate accidents, but as a result of the deeper planning in the mind of God. The effect of the whole process is very clear. Instead of coming, in his adult ministry, from Bethlehem in Judaea, in the heartland of Judaism, Jesus started from the edge, from a place of no reputation or recognition. His ministry started in Galilee, with Galilean people. He moved from Galilee towards Jerusalem, from the edge towards the centre, from people smelling of fish towards people smelling of books. Consider what it would have meant if it had been otherwise. Suppose Jesus had come into Galilee with a posse of literate students, brightly polished from the best schools in Jerusalem, with a message of, 'Hey, you peasants, I've come from headquarters with some good news for you.' He would have simply been fitting into the existing systems of power and influence, bringing perhaps a new message but no really new movement. The movement of Jesus was not a movement which started from the centre and sent ripples out to the edge. It started on the edge and moved towards the centre. This has been the classic pattern of Christian influence, moving, for instance, from the edge of the Roman Empire to its heart. Jesus did not come in on the wings of management. He broke into society under the fringe of management. When, according to Matthew, Jesus did enter Jerusalem, it was the urban sophisticates who were taken by surprise and had to confess their ignorance; it was the Galilean peasantry, who had accompanied Jesus on his southward journey, who were able to say, 'This is Jesus, the prophet from Nazareth in Galilee. We can tell you; he's our home-boy. Whatever you may think of us and our accents, we're here with him; and we are not ashamed of him' (Matthew 21:10–11).

Matthew is telling us that this is the way God works. Bethlehem was not a bad idea. But, in the end, Bethlehem was too important a place to be the taking-off ground for the presence of God in the world. It had to be somewhere in Galilee. And, at the end of the story, that is still where he is to be found (Matthew 28:7 and 10).

Questions for Groups

1. We are becoming increasingly aware of the violence experienced by children, both the violence of individual cruelty and abuse, and the kind of institutionalized violence which causes children to become nomads, to be shunted around from home to home or from bed-sit to bed-sit. Your group could be a place where those who have a painful story to tell can do so without fear or embarrassment.

You could invite a social worker or local councillor to share their concerns about what happens to vulnerable children in your neighbourhood.

2. Do you see the divine pattern, of working from the edge to the centre, taking effect in your church or your area? Where are the new possibilities coming from?

3. Have you had any contact with asylum-seekers or refugees or unwelcome immigrants? What might

happen if your church building was to be claimed as a place of sanctuary?

4. Traditional Church calendars appoint 28 December as the Festival of the Holy Innocents, or Childermas. What ideas can you suggest for this celebration in your local church?

For Prayer and Reflection

This has certainly been the most painful element within this programme of study. It may well have stirred old memories and given new sensitivity to old wounds. In the power of the Christ who has shared some of this sort of experience, be bold in facing these memories. You could look at some of the psalms of lament, such as Psalm 56 and Psalm 88, and write your own psalm to express your own feelings and hopes.

There is a Place

There is a place prepared for little children,
those we once lived for, those we deeply mourn;
those who from play, from learning and from
    laughter
cruelly were torn.

There is a place where hands which held ours
    tightly
now are released beyond all hurt and fear,
healed by that love which also feels our sorrow,
tear after tear.

There is a place where all the lost potential
yields its full promise, finds its true intent;
silenced no more, young voices echo freely
as they were meant.

There is a place where God will hear our
    questions,
suffer our anger, share our speechless grief,
gently repair the innocence of loving
and of belief.

Jesus, who bids us be like little children,
shields those our arms are yearning to embrace.
God will ensure that all are reunited;
there is a place.[2]

Pray for the minority Christian communities in
Egypt, for whom the story of Christ the Refugee is
particularly precious. Also pray for those who are
seeking true peace and justice in the land of Our
Lord's birth, Arab and Israeli, Jew, Christian,
Moslem.

O God, you bring hope out of emptiness, courage out of fear, new life out of grief and loss. Comfort all who have lost their homes, through persecution, war, exile, and deliberate destruction. Bring them back to their homeland, give them security, a place to live, and trustworthy neighbours, so that together they may be a new sign of peace to the world. Amen.[3]

10

In the Temple Again
Luke 2:41–52

Narrator	Every year the parents of Jesus went to Jerusalem for the Passover Festival. When Jesus was twelve years old, they went to the festival as usual. When the festival was over, they started back home, but the boy Jesus stayed in Jerusalem. His parents did not know this; they thought he was with the group, so they travelled a whole day and then started looking for him among their relatives and friends. They did not find him, so they went back to Jerusalem looking for him. On the third day they found him in the Temple, sitting with the Jewish teachers, listening to them and asking questions. All who heard him were amazed at his intelligent answers. His parents were astonished when they saw him, and his mother said to him:
Mary	My son, why have you done this to us? Your father and I have been terribly worried trying to find you.
Narrator	He answered them:
Jesus	Why did you have to look for me? Didn't you know that I had to be in my Father's house?
Narrator	But they did not understand his answer. So Jesus

went back with them to Nazareth, where he
was obedient to them. His mother treasured all
these things in her heart. Jesus grew both in
body and in wisdom, gaining favour with God
and with people.

We return to Luke for a final glimpse of the young Jesus.

Jesus is being brought up faithfully within Jewish custom. Accordingly, at the age of 12 he is approaching
the stage where he becomes *bar-mitzvah*, son of the law.
This was the age at which, in Jewish custom, a boy
could be regarded as a responsible person, able to be
accountable for his actions. He is on the verge of being
a teenager, who would increasingly be claiming indepen-
dence from parents. Up till now, Jesus has been on the
receiving end of other people's initiatives. He has been
born and fed and greeted and blessed and clothed and
washed. But he has also been learning. He has acquired
a wide range of language. Without any conscious act of
his own will, he has grown a hundred thousand million
brain cells. And he has been gradually developing the
skill to handle the extraordinary human equipment
which he inherits along with every other member of the
human race. He has been learning by means of success
and failure, by discovering what behaviour is acceptable
and what is not.

Although the Gospel-writers give us no details about
Jesus' childhood, apart from this one incident, we can
get some idea of his education and formation by noticing
the kind of man he became. Clearly, he grew up to be
a real man, not some sort of human encyclopaedia,

The boy Jesus in the Temple

knowing all the answers without being told. His child-hood has not been spent in hours of meditation on the Mystery of the Blessed Trinity. He also was not the kind of perfectionist for whom there were no moral choices. He had had to learn about choices and about behaviour, like the rest of us. He must have learned by being told off for his mistakes and being affirmed for his achievements.

Suppose we ask, What were Jesus' favourite subjects at school? On the evidence of his mind as we see it in adulthood, there are, in addition to the Scriptures, two subjects which meant most to him – botany and econ-omics. There are very few of his parables which are not centred in these themes, which would include such matters as agricultural practice and land-tenure. If they are put all together, his parables could be used as a basis for a thorough study of socio-economic conditions in the Palestine of his day.

Jesus was learning simply by being part of his culture and community. He did not have to descend to the level of his audiences of peasants; he belonged there.

He was known as the carpenter, or the carpenter's son. Actually, the word translated 'carpenter' means more generally 'builder'. Joseph apparently was the job-bing builder for the village, working mainly in wood; and Jesus would have been learning the same trade. But, in his adult ministry, he does not have much to say about building, and he does not tell stories drawn from that sort of experience. Presumably this is because bot-anical imagery makes sense to almost everyone, whereas fewer people would resonate with illustrations drawn from domestic architecture. (As a trained mechanic turned preacher, I have found the same to be true even in these days.)

The main point here is that, at this stage and all through his life, Jesus was a learner. He worked with the other things of creation and the other inhabitants of the human community. Sometimes, this learning was painful and embarrassing, requiring in him a change of attitude (e.g. Matthew 15:21–28). At other times, it was a matter of grief and disappointment (e.g. Luke 19:41–42). He was known as Teacher; but he showed that one cannot be a teacher unless one is constantly a learner. As the one who discloses what God himself is like, Jesus shows that God also is a learner, working with his infinitely various and complex creation, discovering its potential, adjusting its boundaries.

So we have the learner Jesus aged 12, travelling the sixty-five miles from Nazareth to Jerusalem as a member of the family party of Joseph and Mary. All goes according to plan, until the journey home. Then, disaster. The worst fears of any parent take hold of the hearts of Mary and Joseph. It is easy to be wise after the event, and to say that they ought to have checked more carefully. Up till now, they have been able to rely on their son staying with them without question. Now, either he is no longer reliable or he is the victim of someone else's malice. Which would be worse?

They go back to Jerusalem; only after three anxious days of searching do they find him. He turns out to be quite unable to appreciate their feelings. He assumes that he has the right to mess their lives and their timetables around. A genuine wrong has been done to his caring parents; after all, it is a child's duty, isn't it, not to cause worry. Mary speaks to him in a way which is calculated to make her son feel guilty. He refuses to feel guilty. He has been enjoying the home-from-home experience which Joseph has made possible for him. He has been practising his skill in discussing with religious authorities – a skill which is going to be very necessary in future years. Now he has to negotiate with those to whom he is most closely related. Characteristically, his first utterance is a question. Characteristically, that is, because much of his skill as a teacher will depend on his ability to raise the provocative question. But characteristically, also, because, in a child, no question is more persistent and demanding than the question beginning with 'Why?'

Luke tells us the story as a way of letting us hear the first recorded words of Jesus. Many interpreters read this as a straight claim by Jesus to have a new Father, God, the Lord of the Temple. But Luke's account is not as definite as that. It is not easy to put into English the word of Jesus at this point. Literally, it reads, 'Did you not know that in the things of my father it is necessary for me to be?' Probably the closest translation we can get is: 'Did you not realize that I must be about my father's interests?' This is the version given in the margin of the New Revised Standard Version, and of some other modern versions; it follows the same understanding as the King James version, 'Wist ye not that I must be about my father's business?'

English readers are used to seeing the word 'father', in Mary's words in the previous sentence, spelled with a small 'f', and, immediately afterwards, the same word in the mouth of Jesus spelled with a capital 'F'. So, Mary is talking about Joseph, Jesus is talking about God. But this is interpretation. In Luke's original there was no such distinction between capital letters and small letters; the same is true in many other written languages, particularly Asian languages, and in sign-language. Above all, there is, of course, no such difference in spoken language (trust the English to bring class distinction even into lettering – although I suppose it really goes back to the Romans!) So, Mary clearly refers to Joseph as Jesus' father. Jesus answers that he has been attending to what his father has been wishing him to attend to. He has been in the Temple, the Temple to which Joseph has carefully brought him; and he has been doing in the Temple the things which Joseph has brought him to the Temple to do. He has been fulfilling his father's interests. So, no problem; 'father' is obviously Joseph. Or is he? Christian understanding has not been wrong, all these centuries, in thinking that Jesus is raising the possibility of having an alternative father. But what he says is ambiguous, provocatively ambiguous. In what tone and attitude is Jesus speaking – defiantly, resentfully, patiently, or what? Joseph is left asking himself, Who is he talking about when he talks about his father? Me, or someone else? All right, I did bring him here; I did want him to get a feel of the Temple; but not to make his bed here; not for him to treat it as home; not for him to stay here without us. Does he belong to me any more?

What is the future for Joseph? Who is he any longer?

No wonder Luke tells us that Mary and Joseph did not understand what Jesus meant.

Now some other versions translate the words as '. . . in my Father's house' – rather in the way that we might say, 'I am going to stay at my auntie's.' That would clearly mean that Jesus is claiming that his father is God, the owner of the Temple. But, if Luke had wanted us to understand the words in such a specific way, surely he would have made his meaning more clear and precise. Elsewhere in the Gospels, where Jesus speaks of 'my Father's house', the Greek is quite clear and unambiguous (e.g. John 2:16; 14:2). But here Luke seems to be choosing a deliberately ambiguous expression, for a definite purpose.

Do we conclude that Jesus had two fathers? Why not? His mother, the evangelist, and the general public understand that Jesus' father is Joseph. It is through Joseph that Jesus gets the important title of 'Son of David'. It is through his experience of Joseph's household that Jesus receives his formation as a human being. Later on, as an adult, Jesus certainly addresses God as Father. This gets him into trouble. But it is an essential truth about his own identity. Throughout the Gospels, the question is asked, 'Who are you, where do you come from?' From the moment of the Annunciation to Mary onwards, Luke has been stressing the mysterious double character of Jesus' identity. In this story of Jesus' adolescence, Luke is preparing for this question to appear again and again, with all its mystery and ambiguity. The Church has traditionally answered the same question by teaching that Christ has two natures, divine and human.

Whatever else this may mean, this message at the heart of Christian teaching tells us that Jesus is indeed one of us, *and* that in being one of us he makes an eternal difference to the nature of God.

The idea that God is Father was not a new idea invented by Jesus. It was there in human perception before Jesus came. The inevitable impression from the idea of God as Father is that God is owner, controller, knower, and, above all, that God is adult. We claim that in Christ God takes flesh. God is child. That is the new idea of God made possible by Jesus. For most people, the tensions and struggles against our parents are a major part of our formation through childhood. Parent becomes the enemy to defeat, or the ally to attract, or the punisher to placate, or the supplier to please. Much of our motivation, in both pain and creativity, springs from our position as child in relationship to parent. God is on both sides of the parent/child divide.

In Christ, God shows that he is child as much as he is parent. He is alongside child as much as he is alongside parent. As child, he can wound parent and be led by parent. As parent, he can be taught by child and be responsible for child. In the nature of God as disclosed in Christ, the hostility built into our usual parent–child relationships finds healing. We can face each other across the generation divide without being pulled around by compulsions and fear. Because God in Christ is child, we can honestly and safely pray 'Our Father'.

In this story, Luke is ensuring that we do not merely settle for a baby Jesus; we meet the adolescent Jesus, with all the misunderstandings and puzzlements of adolescence. For him, as for most of us, it is not a steady smooth experience; it involves changes of direction, and new styles of behaviour, and experimenting with new voices. God in Christ knows this from the inside.

The genealogies in Matthew and Luke both stress the importance of Jesus' background and ancestry. He was what his ancestors had made him. So with all of us. He was a Jew, and without his Jewish background he cannot be explained. However, while Jesus was a Jew, not all Jews were Jesus. Any attempt to explain Jesus in terms of environment, economics, religion and so on, will explain the other people of his community as well. But the things which make him most significant are not the ways in which he resembled everyone else around but the ways in which he did not. He was Jesus; others were not. If we are to explain Jesus in terms of his Jewishness, we have also to account for all the ways in which he cannot be explained in terms of his Jewishness. He is more than the product of his heredity. He is more than his racial identity. He is son of Joseph; he is more than son of Joseph. He is Son of David. He is more than Son of David. And the same principle applies to all human beings. Uniqueness will always evade complete analysis.

Racism tells us that the all-important fact about us is where we come from, the unchangeable and unchosen fact of our ancestry. Tell us your colour, your race, your tribe, or your language, and we know who you are; we know how to treat you; we know where you fit into the status-system; we know what you can achieve, what sort of person you can marry, what your children will be like, where you will be buried. We know. Jesus himself was known in this way. Because people knew his family background, they could not believe in him as a teacher (Mark 6:1–6). Knowledge, in this sense, is opposite to faith. Jesus saw people, not in terms of the obvious and unavoidable past, but in terms of a hidden and potential future. So he chose unproven and unreliable people as his disciples. The evangelists are very honest in telling us what a stupid and obstructive lot they often were. If you, as a dedicated and clear-sighted Christian, feel that your colleagues in the congregation, your minister or your bishops, are all pretty thick and disappointing, you are in very good company. Do not worry too much about trying to find some group that will suit you better – you might miss a miracle. Indeed, if you do succeed in finding a church that suits you, you may even succeed in finding a god that suits you, and that really will be an insurance for you against ever having to be changed. There is a potential for you in the future, beyond anything that you can guess. No one else may know about it. But it is already there in the understanding of Jesus.

So Luke is telling us that Jesus, aged 12, was becoming aware of a double parenting. But this was not to be something unique to Jesus. Jesus was to teach that such a double parenting, or new birth, was to be the pattern for all his friends and followers – for instance in John 3:1–8. So he teaches us to pray to God as Father, in the same way as he did. The Church is to be a new family, a family which crosses all the boundaries of language or nation or any other identity. Paul uses the helpful image of the adoptive family, a family of people who do not share the same genetic identity but who are brought together in care and acceptance as different persons in one household (Romans 8:14–17). According to Matthew, this kind of relationship was already built into the experience of the family of Jesus. Joseph was the adoptive father of Jesus; he had given Jesus his family name and his legal status. The Church extends this relationship to us all.

Anyone who has been involved in an adoption procedure will recognize the blessings and demands of the picture of the Church as an adoptive family. Within this family, we are given to each other, and we therefore accept each other because we have already been accepted by Christ (Romans 15:7). Or, as we say more technically in ecclesiastical circles, we are in communion with each other. Our being in communion with each other is not on the basis of our choosing of each other, or our liking each other, or our agreeing with each other. Our choices and our likings and our opinions are mostly formed by the unchosen experiences of the past. We are in communion with each other because Christ is drawing us together into the one community, in which distinction is not destroyed but separation is overcome, as opposites come together. The notion of two natures in one person, which may seem rather abstract as an account of the person of Christ, is in fact a necessary part of the character of every Christian and should be recognizable in the character or every local church. As the old Welsh *plygain* carols put it, Christ is 'ein Brenin gwiw a'n Brawd' – our worthy King and Brother;[1] and that makes a difference to the way we see both the 'kings' and the 'brothers'

– the authority-figures and the family members of our own time and place.

This makes good sense at the theoretical or doctrinal level. But for many of us it is also our straightforward practical experience. Without going in for a lot of theological reflection about it, many of us have found the Church to be a second home in our younger days, have been given second fathers or mothers, have been nourished in alternative families. This may have run us into trouble at home, clashes of timetable, jealousy, tears. Even 'good' children have to distance themselves from 'good' parents. It is all there in the story of the family of Jesus.

Jesus goes back with Joseph and Mary to Nazareth, and takes his place within their home and society. He belongs. He accepts the authority of Mary and Joseph. Luke uses the same word which Paul uses, when he tells the Christians in Rome that they should be 'subject to' the secular authorities (Romans 13:1 – a verse which has been powerfully claimed by ruling groups to keep dissidents in order). It means, to take one's place within the arrangements or the ordering of society. It does not mean servile obedience. It does not rule out being a member of the opposition, or of a Trade Union, or of a movement of conscientious objection. It does mean taking a place responsibly within society, and being willing to accept the penalties which may attach to any defiance. This is a distinction which can be of great importance to people who find themselves called to be a creative opposition within a State. This is how the adolescent Jesus found himself in the household and community of Nazareth. It is not only a statement about his childhood. It is about the meaning of incarnation; if one is truly incarnate, one is at the mercy of the place where one is incarnate. One is alongside the other members of the community, sharing their situation.

This is where Jesus is, and this is how he is where he is. We do not hear anything more about him for another eighteen years or so. He is becoming part of the culture, learning a trade, accepting the conventions of Galilee. 'Creative life is always on the yonder side of convention.' His eighteen hidden years as an adolescent and young adult give him the background for all his teaching. On the far side of being simply a member of the society in which he finds himself, he is able to look the convention direct in the face and challenge it. He earns the right to a hearing. He becomes a disturber from within. When he does make a move, it will be to associate himself with that antique-looking figure, John the Baptist. He will move forward, and downward. He will descend, for baptism, into the lowest part of his country's landscape, the muddy waters of the lower Jordan. Only on the far side of that immersion will he start to disclose the fundamentally new thing that he has to offer.

Meanwhile, he learns the value of Joseph's work and role. He learns the potential sacredness of the various trades and enterprises of his society. He grows in wisdom; this is rather a tame translation of the rare word which Luke uses; it literally means 'he hammered out' his wisdom, and his peaceful relationship with God and with other people. His spiritual growth and his social growth go hand in hand. His religious awareness does not keep him childish; his involvement with people keeps pace with his involvement with God.

Questions for Groups

1. Divide the group into three teams, one to look at the experience of Joseph and Mary, one to look at the experience of Jesus, and one to look at the role of the teachers in the Temple. Each team asks itself, What are our feelings in the course of this story? What are our responsibilities? What do we feel about the other characters in the story with whom we have to relate? After ten minutes or so of getting into the roles, let each team send off one or two members to visit one of the other teams, to face the question, What do you think of us? What has been the effect of our behaviour on you? (If possible, it might be good to have young people taking the part of the parents and older people taking the part of Jesus.)

After working on these questions, let each team clarify its feelings and ideas. Then come together, and look at such questions as:

How far is your church supporting young people at this sort of stage? Does it represent God who is on the side of the child as well as God who is on the side of the parent? How far is your church a kind of alternative home for young people? Does it give the impression of being simply an extension of parents' authority, or does it enable young people to have a voice of their own?

2. As you come to the end of this study-programme, make arrangements to assemble the various ideas for further study and action which may have emerged. Put them into some order of priority. Decide on things that can be done in the next six months, in the next year, or in the next three years. Be honest about things which just have to be left on one side for the time being. Who are you going to speak to? What approaches are you going to make to your lay leadership, your minister or parish priest, your bishop or superintendent, your local authority, your MP, your local press, or whoever else?

For Prayer and Reflection

'Sunday after Sunday, I listen in vain (usually) for the work-places and work problems of the congregation to figure in the intercessions. We go regularly on a Cook's Tour of the trouble spots of the globe, but of the trouble spots of the local factory or supermarket there is alas no mention.'[2] Is this true of your congregation? Can you start to make your prayer, and the prayer of your church, more local and more related to the work which sustains the fabric of the community?

Creed of Radical Christ

Leader: Let us declare our trust in Christ.
All: I trust myself to Jesus Christ.

Group One	*Group Two*
Son of a carpenter	
	Calling God Father
One with his people	
	Creating a new family
Draining the old wine	
	Fermenting the new
Open to everyone	
	Narrowing the gate
Deliverer of captives	
	Binding the free
Bringer of peace	
	Stirring up strife
Creator of unity	
	Dividing asunder
Hope for the hopeless	
	Disappointing many hopes
Crucified for all	
	Calling cross-bearers

Emptying the tomb

> Going ahead of us

All: I trust myself through this Jesus
To the Kingdom he points to,
To the Father behind it,
In the Spirit who sustains it,
With disciples everywhere who live for it.[3]

Notes and Acknowledgements

Bible passages are quoted from *The Dramatised Bible* and from the *Good News Bible*, published by the Bible Society.

The title of this book is taken from Phillips Brooks, no 32 in *The New English Hymnal* (Norwich, Canterbury Press, 1986).

Introduction

1 Questions of historical accuracy and significance are thoroughly dealt with in Hugh Montefiore, *The Womb and the Tomb* (London, HarperCollins, 1992). I refer to 'Matthew' and 'Luke' as the names traditionally given to the authors of the Gospels which are printed normally in first and third positions in the New Testament. I accept that 'Luke' probably was written by Luke the companion of Paul, who also wrote the Acts of the Apostles. The author of 'Matthew' seems to have been someone whose identity is unknown to us, but who had a special interest in the message of Jesus as the new Moses and the fulfiller of Israel's hopes.

Chapter 1

1 A. J. P. Taylor. See Donald Nicholl *The Beatitude of Truth* (London, Darton, Longman and Todd, 1997), p. 95.

Chapter 2

1 Kenneth Leech, *True God* (London, Sheldon Press, 1985), p. 383. See also Kenneth Leech, *The Social God* (London, Sheldon Press, 1981), especially pp. 25–38.

2 George F. MacLeod, *Only One Way Left* (Glasgow, Iona Community, 1956), p. 70.

3 John L. Bell, *Innkeepers and Light Sleepers* (Glasgow, Wild Goose Publications, Iona Community, 1992), p. 27, quoted here with permission. A cassette of these songs is also published.

Chapter 3

1 Karl Gaspar, quoted in *Your Will be Done* (Singapore, Christian Conference of Asia, 1984), p. 8.

2 See Chapter 6, note 1.

3 Edward Cox, in *Seeing Christ in Others* (Norwich, Canterbury Press, 1998), p. 32.

Chapter 4

1 C. G. Jung, *The Integration of the Personality* (London, Kegan Paul, 1940), p. 295.

2 A chant for the words *Wait for the Lord* . . . can be found in *Songs and Prayers from Taizé* (London, Geoffrey Chapman Mowbray, 1991), p. 43.

Chapter 5

1 See E. Martin Browne (ed.), *Religious Drama 2: Mystery and Morality Plays* (New York, Meridian Books, 1958), pp. 102ff.

2 Patrick Thomas, *Candle in the Darkness* (Llandysul, Gwasg Gomer, 1993), p. 110.

3 A. M. Allchin, *The World is a Wedding* (London, Darton, Longman and Todd, 1978), p. 57.

4 Copyright Meic Stephens from *Collected Poems of Harri Webb* (by permission of Gwasg Gomer, Llandysul).

5 I owe this story to my predecessor at Llanrhaeadr, the Revd David Francis, Borth. See also Chapter 10, note 1.

6 A. M. Allchin, *Praise Above All* (Cardiff, University of Wales Press, 1991), pp. 98–9. Quoted here by permission of Canon Allchin. See also the Nativity songs in the Wild Goose publication *Innkeepers and Light Sleepers*, of which there are examples elsewhere in this book.

7 E. Milner-White, *After the Third Collect* (London, Mowbray, 1952), p. 88. Permission from the holders of copyright, the Friends of York Minster.

Chapter 6

1 The songs Magnificat and Nunc Dimittis have inspired a wonderful range of musical interpretation; but it would appear that some composers are more concerned than others to recognize and express the underlying theological and dramatic structure of the texts. Among these versions which do seem to take this structure seriously are Herbert Howells' *Collegium Regale* and *Gloucester* services, Stanford in G, and Dyson in F. Howells especially seems to me to catch the immense range of spiritual drama which the texts represent. I am grateful to my son-in-law, Gareth Price, and to Bishop Kenneth Skelton, for advice in this exploration.

2 For the reasoning behind this proposal, and a more detailed text, see Hugh Montefiore, *On Being a Jewish Christian* (London, Hodder & Stoughton, 1998), pp. 15–40. Text quoted here by permission of Bishop Montefiore.

3 Uniting Church in Australia, National Commission for Mission; in Geoffrey Duncan (ed.), *Seeing Christ in Others* (Norwich, Canterbury Press, 1998), p. 220.

4 From Janet Morley, Hannah Ward, and Jennifer Wild, *Dear Life* (London, Christian Aid, 1998), by permission.

Chapter 7

1 A. M. Allchin, *God's Presence Makes the World* (London, Darton, Longman and Todd, 1997), p. 148.

2 See Richard Beadle and Pamela M. King (eds.), *York Mystery Plays* (Oxford, Clarendon Press, 1984), pp. 48ff., the play *Joseph's Trouble with Mary*.

3 Adapted from Tom Colvin, *Christ the Worker*, in *Fill us with your Love* (copyright by Hope Publishing Co., Carol Stream, Illinois, 60188, USA, 1969), p. 9. Text includes music. All rights reserved. Used by permission of Tom Colvin and Publishers.

Chapter 8

1 See, for instance, the picture in the National Gallery, *The Adoration of the Magi*, by Pieter Bruegel the Elder (sixteenth century). The Magi represent the three main races of humankind; they seem to be rich but puzzled people. The Mother and Child are surrounded by signs of poverty, confusion and violence, by uncomprehending peasants and armed soldiers. It is very much the real world of the artist's day and of Matthew's story.

2 References are to Ignatius of Antioch, *Letter to the*

Ephesians 19:3; Justin, *Dialogue* 78, 9: cited in W. K. Lowther Clarke, *Divine Humanity* (London, SPCK, 1936), p. 43, and C. S. Mann OSB in *Theology*, December 1958, p. 496. Full text of Ignatius reference in Staniforth and Louth, *Early Christian Writings* (Harmondsworth, Penguin, 1987), p. 66.

3 Peter Selby, *Grace and Mortgage* (London, Darton, Longman & Todd, 1997), p. 107. It's worth noting, in passing, that the Commissioners got into trouble because of unsuccessful investment in property, which is another way of describing speculation in the movement of land values, a form of speculation which is very likely to operate to the disadvantage of the poorest owner-occupiers.

4 Extract from G. K. Chesterton, *The Ballad of the White Horse*, in *Poems for All Purposes*, ed. Stephen Medcalf (London, Pimlico, 1994), p. 106; quoted here by permission of A. P. Watt Ltd on behalf of The Royal Literary Fund.

5 John L. Bell, *Innkeepers and Light Sleepers*, p. 51. See Chapter 2, note 3 above.

6 Tropar of the Ukrainian Liturgy of the Nativity; quoted in Geo T. Montague, *Companion God* (New Jersey, Paulist Press, 1989). Quoted here by permission of the Paulist Press.

Chapter 9

1 *The Poems of Wilfred Owen*, edited by Jon Stallworthy (London, Hogarth Press, 1985), p. 151. Quoted here by permission of Professor Stallworthy.

2 John L. Bell and Graham Maule, *When Grief is Raw* (Glasgow, Wild Goose Publications, Iona Community, 1997), p. 92. This song was written in memory of the sixteen primary school children and their teacher who were killed by a gunman at 9.30 a.m. on Wednesday 13 March 1996, in Dunblane, Scotland. Quoted here by permission.

3 From Palestinian Remembrance Service at Westminster

Cathedral, 2 May 1998, published in *Living Stones* magazine (St Mary's University College, Twickenham), number 16, autumn 1998. By permission of *Living Stones* magazine.

Chapter 10

1 Geraint Vaughan-Jones, *Hen Garolau Plygain* (Talybont, Y Lolfa, 1987), p. 27. Similar phrases occur in several other carols in the book.

2 Bishop Michael Henshall in Bernard Braley (ed.), *Touching the Pulse: Worship and where we Work* (London, Stainer & Bell, 1996), p. 78.

3 John J. Vincent (ed.), *Community Worship* (Sheffield, Ashram Community Trust, 1987), p. 52: reproduced here by permission of the Publisher/Author.